Sexy CITY cocktails

Stylish Drinks & Cool Classics
You Can Sip with Attitude

Sheree Bykofsky and Megan Buckley

Adams Media Corporation
Avon, Massachusetts

For Karen, who did the research with us.
And for Pat Buckley, who knows that some things in life
are all froth and no Guinness. —MB

Published by
Adams Media, an F+W Publications Company
57 Littlefield Street, Avon, MA 02322. U.S.A.
www.adamsmedia.com

ISBN: 1-58062-917-2

Printed in Canada.

J I H G F E D C

Library of Congress Cataloging-in-Publication Data
Bykofsky, Sheree.
Sexy city cocktails / by Sheree Bykofsky and Megan Buckley.
p.   cm.
Includes index.
ISBN 1-58062-917-2
1. Cocktails. 2. Non-alcoholic cocktails. I. Buckley, Megan.
II. Title.
TX951.B789   2003
641.8'74--dc21   2003001033

This publication is designed to provide accurate and authoritative information with
regard to the subject matter covered. It is sold with the understanding that the
publisher is not engaged in rendering legal, accounting, or other professional advice.
If legal advice or other expert assistance is required, the services of a competent
professional person should be sought.
        —From a *Declaration of Principles* jointly adopted by a Committee of the
American Bar Association and a Committee of Publishers and Associations

Many of the designations used by manufacturers and sellers to distinguish their
products are claimed as trademarks. Where those designations appear in this
book and Adams Media was aware of a trademark claim, the designations have
been printed with initial capital letters.

Please enjoy alcoholic beverages responsibly, and only if you're of legal age.

This book is available at quantity discounts for bulk purchases.
For information, call 1-800-872-5627.

Contents

ACKNOWLEDGMENTS

*W*e couldn't have done it without you! Karen Hassey; Ken Jacobson; Molly "Ryan" McGuire; the vigilant Laura Goldstein; Janet Rosen, who's famous even though she's not a man; Katharine Sands (this book's "godmother"); editor extraordinaire Jill Alexander; Glenn Chu; mixologist Erin Sullivan; fashionista Kamil Fulwood; restauranteur Xania Woodman; the inspirational Sandra McGowan; Rochester correspondent Joanna Wulfsberg; Karen Buckley, who thinks Mother's Day is sexy; "researchers" Dona Burke and Kathleen Junge; ultra-romantic Susan Hassey; and the wonderfully patient staff of Fitzgerald's Pub in Manhattan, especially Kevin, Denis Sr., Eoin, Roger, and Hergit.

INTRODUCTION

$\mathcal{W}$hen you watch the bartenders at your favorite bar mix up fabulous cocktails, you probably wonder, "How do they do that?" Bartenders know how to make magnificent martinis, luscious margaritas, and other spectacular creations appear almost magically before your eyes—and they make it look so easy!

That's because it is! Girls, you don't have to spend lots of cash at swank, pricey places to enjoy great cocktails—instead, you can become a mistress of mixology, and make them yourself! Whether you're throwing the biggest party of the year, inviting the girls over for a few drinks before heading out for a night on the town, or staging a romantic tête-à-tête with your new flame, you'll find just the drink you're thinking of in *Sexy City Cocktails*. And we've jam-packed the margins with fun, helpful facts; you'll love our tips for creating great ambience, beating morning-after headaches, how not to end up on the back of some guy's motorcycle at 2 A.M., and lots more.

What do you need to get your very own bar started? It's simple! Just keep the following basics on hand.

One bottle each of:
- Vodka
- Triple sec

- Tequila
- Light rum
- Amaretto or Frangelico
- Champagne

And:
- Plenty of ice!
- Fruit juices, such as orange and cranberry
- Grenadine
- Lemons, limes, maraschino cherries, and other fruit for garnish

Plus barware:
- Cocktail shaker
- Strainer
- Blender
- Cocktail glasses
- Collins glasses
- Old-Fashioned glasses
- Wine glasses
- Champagne flutes

Then add other ingredients—such as flavored vodkas or liqueurs—as you need them. Be creative!

So break out the blender, fire up your cocktail shaker, and read on. In no time, you'll be the hottest hostess in town!

Chapter 1
The Timelessly Tempting Martini

ou've got the perfect little Prada dress. You splurged on those blade-thin stilettos by Manolo, and you don't regret a thing. Because by now, you've got time for one more drink (back at your place) and you offer him a martini. He falls at your feet. Why? Because "May I mix you a martini?" says, "I've got class. I know what I want, and I want it straight up, with or without a twist, baby."

You know you want a martini, and there are so many different ways to have it; from citrusy to savory, with everything from chocolate to curaçao. Try an original clear-as-water Gin Martini if you're feeling sleek and chic, a sweet and tart Sea Breezetini if you'd rather be on the beach, or a luscious Toasted Hazelnut Martini for lickable lips. And no matter what your poison, what's *not* sexy when sipped from a martini glass? Nothing!

So whether you want to ask him back to your place or you and the girls are getting ready to paint the town red, these recipes are guaranteed to spice up any night or sweeten a tête-à-tête. Get ready to seduce and be seduced!

VODKA MARTINI

*M*artinis are so back in style, along with all things decadent, such as cigars and deliciously fattening foods (and these are a few of our favorite things!). In spite of endless, fabulous variations on this theme, the original simply can't be beat. These days, many omit the vermouth entirely; while some still prefer just a tinge of vermouth's sweetness. It's simply a matter of taste. Either way, it's timeless.

3 ounces vodka (try chilling it first to give it extra bite!)
⅛–¼ teaspoon dry vermouth
1 lemon twist or green cocktail olive (or any garnish that tickles your taste buds, such as fruit slices, fruit zest, or bitters)

Some like to omit the vermouth altogether in favor of the vodka's smoothness—but we like the classic recipe. Mix vodka and vermouth with ice in a cocktail shaker or mixing glass, then strain into a chilled cocktail glass. Slip a twist of lemon over the edge of the glass, and find out why the martini's timeless!

HE'S ONE OF THE MOST FAMOUS MARTINI DRINKERS IN HISTORY—AND HE'S sexy to boot. Too bad he's not a real guy! He's Bond, James Bond, and he likes his Vodka Martinis stirred, not shaken. Seems to have gotten him the girl every time, from Tiffany Case to Honey Rider to the famously named Pussy Galore. If it got him the girl, it'll get you the guy—try a martini 007-style! Stir the vodka and vermouth after pouring it over ice, then gently strain into a sparkling glass.

GIN MARTINI

*A*h, juniper. Here's why some martini drinkers love a Gin Martini, and others must have vodka: while the latter is practically tasteless (and therefore quite versatile), the former's got the definitive bite of the juniper berries from which it's made. We love it—especially with a briny cocktail olive to complement its kick. You'll be a convert to the Gin Martini in no time!

3 ounces gin
$\frac{1}{4}$ teaspoon dry vermouth or less, to taste
1 green cocktail olive or lemon twist

Pour gin and vermouth over ice in a tall mixing glass. Stir gently and then slowly swirl into a chilled cocktail glass. Finish with a jaunty twist of lemon, or pop a classic cocktail olive (or 2) into the mix. Perfection!

IF YOU LIKE YOUR MARTINI DRY—THAT IS, WITH AS LITTLE VERMOUTH AS POSsible—try this extra dash of extravagance: Instead of adding vermouth to the mix at all, simply spritz it over your 'tini with a perfume atomizer. (You can buy an actual vermouth atomizer at specialty shops and Web sites, but that wouldn't be as much fun, would it?)

THE TIMELESSLY TEMPTING MARTINI

Dirty Martini

Bad girl! This flavorful twist on the martini muddles the waters by adding olive juice to the mix, along with a couple of whole olives floating at the bottom of the glass. If you like all things salty, you'll love an extra olive-juicy Dirty Martini—if not, add just a drop or two of olive brine. D.M.'s are especially delicious with raw seafood . . . and you know what they say about oysters . . .

3 ounces gin	½ ounce olive brine
½–1 ounce vermouth	Lots of green cocktail olives

Over cracked ice, combine the gin, vermouth, and olive brine. (Pop an olive into your date's mouth with your fingertips.) Shake it up, and pour into a cold, cold cocktail glass. Slip as many olives as you like on a toothpick, and rest it on the rim of the glass (if you can resist eating them!).

WHEN BARTENDER JERRY THOMAS WHIPPED UP A MARTINEZ COCKTAIL AT THE Occidental Hotel in the late 1800s, who'd have thought it would've taken off like a shot (of vodka, that is)? What started out as a simple, slightly sweet cocktail has become the height of fashion in any form, from fruity to dirty, and garnished with everything from orange slices to olives stuffed with bleu cheese. So experiment! Jerry would be proud.

BLUE MOON MARTINI

Don't wait to have one of these until you see the real deal hanging in the sky! They're too pretty to drink only once in a blue moon. Essentially, this is a classic Gin Martini—blue gin and blue curaçao give it a bold, deep blue hue without really altering its taste. One caveat: Skip the olives in favor of a twist, even if you're a die-hard olive-martini girl; the orange or lemon peel twisted over the edge of this true-blue drink is stunning.

2½ ounces Bombay Sapphire gin
Dash of vermouth, or to taste
¼ ounce blue curaçao
1 orange or lemon twist (a piece of peel cut into a long thin swirl)

Those baby blues! Stir all but the orange peel into a mixing glass with plenty of ice, then strain into a chilled cocktail glass. Loop the orange peel over the edge, sit back, and wait for your date to tell you your eyes are the color of a . . . martini?

"One martini is all right. Two are too many, and three are not enough." —James Thurber
Sounds like a good idea at the time, but if you don't keep yourself in check you may end up on the back of some guy's motorcycle skidding around the streets of Manhattan at 2 A.M. praying for a red light. (Um, not that anything like that has ever happened to us . . .) So sip slowly!

Apple Martini

We love drinks—and men—that are flexible, and in that category the martini is number one! Vodka is the perfect complement to all kinds of liqueurs, especially fruits like apple, banana, raspberry, and more. Don't try these with gin, though—its fresh, one-of-a-kind taste will clash with the subtlety and sweetness of the fruit. The Apple Martini is Sheree's favorite! We don't want to make any guarantees, but whenever she's ordered these on dates—even blind ones—the night's been one to remember. Coincidence? We think not.

1 lemon slice
3 ounces vodka
1 ounce apple schnapps
Cinnamon sugar, to rim glass
1–2 apple slices dipped in lemon juice, for garnish

Moisten rim of cocktail glass with a lemon slice. Combine vodka and apple schnapps over ice in your handy mixing glass. Pour a few teaspoonfuls of cinnamon sugar onto a plate, then shake gently to even out. Dip rim of glass and coat evenly. Pour mixed liquor into the cocktail glass and slip a thin apple slice over the rim to finish. (Dip apple slices in lemon juice first so they stay fresh and crisp.)

Banana Martini

*T*ropically sexy, this yummy variation on the martini theme is one of the smoothest we've ever had. (And trust us, we've had many.) The banana liqueur, which can be overpoweringly sweet when its powers are used for evil, is offset by the vodka's clear crispness. By the way, what do bananas make *you* think of?

2½–3 ounces vodka or vanilla vodka
1–1½ ounces banana liqueur
1 lemon twist, for garnish
1 lime twist, for garnish

Starting with the vodka, pour ingredients over the rocks in a mixing glass. Shake well—it's all in the wrist—and strain every last drop into a chilled cocktail glass. Then slide one lemon and lime twist each over the rim of the glass. Lip-licking good.

PEAR MARTINI

*A*lthough this is a recipe you won't find behind most bars, it's the perfect treat for lengthening a late summer night. If you don't want to invest in a whole bottle of pear schnapps, try pear nectar instead (even though it may sound exotic, you should be able to find it in most major supermarkets). It's just as good, but it'll dilute the vodka a bit. Mix up a double for the romantic *tête-à-tête* you've been planning for you and your man.

2–2½ ounces vodka
1–1½ ounces pear schnapps, or pear nectar
2–3 mint sprigs, for garnish

Swirl that vodka and pear schnapps (or pear nectar) together over ice in a mixing glass. After shaking well, strain into a martini glass, and pop in a mint sprig. Sip. Sip. Repeat. Cooling off yet? Or are things just beginning to heat up?

SEA BREEZETINI

$\mathcal{T}$he old standby, the Sea Breeze, has gotten a thoroughly modern makeover! This sexy summery drink is a great prelude to your next GNO (Girls, Night Out), and a no-fuss addition to any party, since it's so easy to make at home. Or ask that hot bartender at your favorite nightspot to mix one for you; if he doesn't know how, you'll have to give him private lessons.

1½ ounce citrus vodka (such as Absolut Citron)
½ ounce Campari
½ ounce red grapefruit juice
½ ounce cranberry juice
1 slice of lime or other citrus wedge

Mix 'em up in a cocktail shaker on the rocks, shake and shake, then strain into a martini glass. Add a twist of lime or a slice of citrus for a flirtatious, fruity libation.

WHAT'S CAMPARI? IT'S A SLIGHTLY BITTER APERITIF WINE, GREAT FOR ADDING a tease of tartness to otherwise sweet drinks, and has been hailed as the height of elegance in Italy and other European countries since the turn of the century. Try it over club soda, too.

New York is so swank, and Manhattan boasts some of the most glamorous, elegant bars in the United States, and even the world, and many of them make a smashing martini. Some of our favorite places to meet, sip, and linger are:

- **Temple Bar**—332 Lafayette Street, (212) 925-4242. This well-kept secret is an elegant, impressive hideaway in Soho. Now that the word's out, you too can stop in and try a fabulous Apple Martini!

- **Pravda**—281 Lafayette Street, (212) 226-4696. When we hit Pravda during the summer there was a longish line outside, but it was worth the wait for their Chocolate Martini with a chocolate-covered strawberry on the rim. Pravda's intimate little tables and basement location give it an insiders-only, clandestine feeling. Try all of their 70 types of vodka!

- **Cibar**—56 Irving Place, (212) 460-5656. The loveseats by the fireplace or the hidden bamboo garden in back—it's a tough choice! You'll have trouble deciding between Cibar's 23 martini blends, too—but you can't go wrong when you bring a date to this Gramercy-area boîte.

INCREDIBLE APRICOT INFUSION

*P*laces like the Russian Vodka Room in Manhattan, or Fire and Ice in Cambridge, Massachusetts, feature mouth-watering glass jars of fruits and herbs steeping in top-of-the-line vodka. Who knew it could be so easy to create your own? All you need is 24 to 48 hours, some easy-to-find fruits, vegetables, or herbs (though we think fruits work best) and a bottle of good vodka (we like Stoli or Grey Goose). Bang! Instant martini!

12 dried apricots, diced
1 liter vodka

Drop diced apricots into vodka, recap bottle, and keep in a relatively dark space for 24 hours. Turn occasionally so apricot flavor will be even throughout the bottle. Taste for flavor, then strain into a new bottle or container. Store in freezer or refrigerator; you've got an instant cocktail! But don't let it sit around for too long; it's best if used in about 3 months. What a great excuse to have another drink!

HOT AND SPICY GINGER INFUSION

As with Incredible Apricot Infusion, you can use your homemade ginger vodka to create martinis or other exotic concoctions of your own, or you can simply serve them straight up in a small glass carafe with cordial or shot glasses. But beware! Since you're drinking straight liquor, you'll want to alternate these with water; otherwise, you might find yourself dancing on the bar before 6 P.M. (Yes, we speak from experience.)

1½-inch piece fresh gingerroot, diced
1 liter vodka

Pop diced ginger into vodka bottle, recap, and place in a dark space for about 48 hours. Turn once in a while to mix ginger and vodka well. Strain into a new bottle and store in freezer. Like apricot-infused vodka, it's best if used within 3 months. Cheers!

"I like to have a martini,
Two at the very most;
Three I'm under the table;
Four I'm under my host!"
—Dorothy Parker

Chocolate Martini

Sin is in! We love this combination of our two favorite vices. It works well as an ending to the perfect evening, or to start it out with a subtle bang. If you're stuck on sweets, try it with something equally as rich and chocolaty, like a chocolate soufflé or chocolate mousse. For something a little lighter, fresh berries and whipped cream will do the trick.

3 ounces vodka
1 ounce chocolate liqueur (such as Godiva)
Cocoa powder, to rim glass
1–2 chocolate candy kisses, or a couple of cocoa beans, for garnish

Try not to finish the chocolate liqueur before you even get to the martini! Pour the vodka, ice, and chocolate liqueur in your mixing glass, shake, and strain heaven into a cocktail glass. Dust the rim with cocoa powder, or blow a chocolate kiss or a couple of cocoa beans into your date's drink. Decadence!

"If you are not feeling well, if you have not slept, chocolate will revive you. But you have no chocolate! I think of that again and again! My dear, how will you ever manage?" —Marquise de Sevigne

Sheree's Vanilla Vampire

ere's to creativity! When Sheree added a few drops of blood-red raspberry Chambord to simple vanilla vodka, she really put the "vamp" into vampire—and invented a whole new martini! With just two basic ingredients, this deep red cocktail is a must-do for your single-ladies-only Valentine's Day party—forget the men for a night, invite the girls over, and indulge in Vanilla Vampires galore.

3 ounces vanilla vodka
½–1 ounce Chambord
Fresh raspberries

Pour vodka over cracked ice, shake, and strain into a cocktail glass. Drizzle ½ ounce Chambord (or to taste) into chilled vodka. Drop 1 fresh raspberry into glass and let it settle on the bottom—when your drink is gone, the raspberry is the best part!

Toasted Hazelnut Martini

*A*fter you've tasted this little number, you'll know why Italians love to add Frangelico—hazelnut liqueur—to their after-dinner coffee and sip small glasses of it straight. Yes, hazelnut adds such a creamy, sultry, sweet-and-nutty taste to anything from coffee to chocolate to martinis—Megan couldn't resist mixing it with a little Stoli Vanil. *Voilà!*

3 ounces vanilla vodka
1 ounce hazelnut liqueur, such as Frangelico
Hazelnuts for garnish (if you really feel like going all out!)

Toss the vodka and the hazelnut liqueur into a cocktail shaker over ice. Shake well so that the flavors are perfectly mixed, then carefully strain into a chilled cocktail glass. Float a whole hazelnut on top, and get ready to go nuts!

A TRADITIONAL MOJITO IS A FRESH, CITRUSY DRINK MADE WITH LIGHT RUM, fresh mint leaves muddled in sugar, and lime juice. It's the perfect cooler for a hot summer day—or a hot summer date! Try our recipe on page 52.

Mojito Martini

hen the classic martini meets this trendy Latin-inspired cooler, the result is a killer combination that'll have you ready to salsa! This luscious libation is worth a little bit of advance preparation. At least two days before making the Mojito Martini, place 2 ounces of fresh mint in a bottle of limon rum. And you can make simple syrup in a snap by melting 2 cups of sugar in 1 cup of water and letting it cool. Serve these up at your next fiesta with grilled shrimp, chips, and spicy salsa with jalapeño.

1 mint leaf
1 ounce simple syrup (see page 58 for complete recipe)
2 ounces mint-infused limon rum
2 ounces freshly squeezed lime juice

Hemingway loved it; you will, too. First, stick a fresh mint leaf to the inside rim of a chilled cocktail glass by placing a drop of simple syrup on it. Then, combine the rest of the simple syrup with all the other ingredients in a cocktail shaker, add ice and shake well (at least 10 times) to ensure that the flavors of lime and mint-lemony rum are in harmony. Strain into glass: then put your dancing shoes on, and grab a guy for the merengue!

$\mathcal{W}$ell, there you have it, girls: From the classic to the contemporary, the martini has come way, way back in style. Why? Because it's just so versatile, there's a yummy version for everyone. Whether you're craving a no-nonsense Dirty Martini (three olives, please!) or a fabulously frou-frou Sea Breezetini, there's bound to be a variation that tickles your fancy. And nothing's more fun than mixing and matching to create your very own signature drink. Since vodka's such a chameleon, you can't go wrong. Serve up your original concoction at your next party—it's guaranteed to impress!

CHAPTER 2
CHAMPAGNE CHIC

C hampagne—it's sex in a bottle. It's decadence, celebration, romance, and desire. It's the epitome of elegance—the height of sophistication. There's no better way to make your night a starry one than by popping open a bottle of the bubbly!

Of course, champagne is a treat all on its own. But these flirty, fruity, sweet, and spicy cocktails add sparkle and style to any girls' night out, romantic rendezvous, or even brunch the next morning. Now, a word to the wise: it's tempting, especially when you're on a budget (and who isn't?), but skip the 3-for-$10 bottles and splurge a little on a decent bottle of champers. There are plenty of great $8–$15 bottles available at just about any liquor store. We especially like Freixenet. (Don't try to pronounce it—just drink it.)

So don't wait until New Year's to treat yourself. After you've tried the Cherry Pop, the French 69, and the Mimosa Kiss, we know you won't want to!

CHAMPAGNE COCKTAIL

*I*magine you're sitting across from Bogart at an intimate little table in *Casablanca* with this classic twist on the bubbly—heaven, no? It's an elegant way to start out dinner for two, and if you're indulging in an intimate evening in, it's just the thing. (If you're out and about, be a showoff and order one with appetizers. You might even teach the bartender a thing or two!)

1 sugar cube
Few dashes of bitters (such as Angostura, Peychaud's, or orange)
4–5 ounces champagne
1 lemon peel

Pop a sugar cube into the bottom of a champagne flute and get it nice and wet with bitters. Fill glass with cold champagne (you'll want to lick any spilled drops off the table—or your date). Twirl a lemon peel over the edge—and start your evening out right.

PAIR CHOCOLATE-COVERED STRAWBERRIES WITH ANY CHAMPAGNE DRINK FOR A decadent, lip-licking touch. They're so easy to make, too! You'll need a dozen large ripe strawberries and ½ pound of your favorite chocolate, coarsely chopped. Melt the chocolate in a saucepan over a low, low flame (stir often). Dip the berries in the chocolate one at the time, then lay them on waxed paper to cool. Pop them in the fridge, but make sure to eat them within a day or they'll lose their freshness.

French 69

Okay, so it's traditionally called the French 75—but those six degrees of separation make it so much sexier! Lemon juice mixed with cognac or gin gives champagne a bite that can't be beat. Invest in some quality cognac, and treat yourself and that significant someone to the classiest of cocktails. For extra style, rim the glass with sugar and pop a lemon slice over the edge.

1 ounce lemon juice
½–¾ ounce simple syrup (see page 58 for directions)
1½ ounces cognac or gin
4–5 ounces brut champagne

Swirl lemon juice and simple syrup in a chilled Collins glass until syrup is completely dissolved. Add cognac or gin, fill with cold champagne, and stir very, very gently (to twist the words of Mr. Bond a bit, all drinks made with champagne should be stirred, not shaken).

THE BEST PARTY MEGAN EVER THREW WAS A CHAMPAGNE AND CHOCOLATE party. Months later it was still being talked about! You'll be infamous, too, if you invest in a few decent bottles of bubbly and some class-A chocolate (see page 92 for our fave chocolate recommendations. It's that easy!).

KIR ROYALE

It's oh-so-simple to make, and the cassis—currant liqueur—sweetens champagne perfectly. A staple in bars and restaurants all over Europe, from Parisian cafés to German pubs, the Kir Royale is regaining speed in the United States these days, too, after being forgotten for a bit. Be your trendsetting self and mix up a few! It's an easy way to add sparkle to any party.

6 ounces brut champagne
½ ounce crème de cassis

Fill a champagne flute with champagne, then carefully add the cassis. Twirl the glass a few times to mix—it's all in the wrist, you know—and *voilà!*

UNLIKE VERSATILE VODKA, INFUSING CHAMPAGNE AT HOME IS NEXT TO IMPOSsible. Once you open a bottle of bubbly, it really should be consumed immediately (a great excuse to have one more glass—it's true!) or it'll lose its signature fizz. If you're prowling about at a champagne bar, though, or a bar of the caliber of, say, the Russian Tea Room in New York, look for incredible infusions such as lavender or ginger. You can make the next-best thing by muddling a bit of the herb or fruit at the bottom of a glass, which releases its essential oils and flavors.

Champagne Snap

*G*inger—it's not all sugar and spice anymore. (Remember the long-lashed tropical transplant of the same name on *Gilligan's Island?*) This wicked cocktail pairs vodka with champagne, giving each sip a bigger bang. Plus, the vodka helps bring out the ginger's flavor. Don't be afraid to alter our recommended amount of ginger to taste—add three slivers instead of two if you like your drink nice and spicy; add a half or one sliver for a more muted taste.

2 thin slivers gingerroot   4 ounces champagne
1 ounce vodka

Slide ginger and vodka into the bottom of a cocktail shaker. Use the tip of a wooden spoon to muddle the mixture (see page 60). Now fill the glass with ice and shake well. Strain into a chilled champagne flute and top of with champagne . . . as much as you'd like.

NAMED FOR ONE OF THE SEXIEST, MOST POWERFUL WOMEN IN HISTORY, THE wide-mouthed champagne glasses—like the ones you see in old movies and their cheap cousins, the plastic ones you see in grocery stores—are called Cleopatra glasses. Legend has it that they were created in the shape of her breasts, but, in fact, they were modeled after Princess Eugénie's décolletage. (Stick with champagne flutes for their narrower shape—the shallow, wide shape of the Cleopatra glass allows the champagne to lose its chill too quickly.)

BELLINI

You're rehashing every detail of Saturday night over Sunday brunch. Skip the mimosa this time, and whip up a few of these crisp, sweet eye-openers. (Of course, they're perfect as predinner drinks, too!) A few years ago, Bellinis were rarely seen on the scene; now they're making a comeback, often as specialty drinks, in classy bars and restaurants everywhere. We've even spotted frozen Bellinis here and there!

2 ounces peach nectar
1 ounce fresh lemon juice
3 ounces brut champagne

Pour fruit juices into a chilled champagne flute, add champagne, and swirl or stir gently. (We like to substitute 1 ounce of the peach nectar with 1 ounce of peach schnapps, which is a little too bold for brunch, but perfect for the P.M.!)

Raspberry Risqué

Ooh, Chambord. That gorgeous pink color and lip-licking raspberry taste go well with just about anything. Here, it transforms simple champagne and vodka into a hot little number that cools so well. Plus, it's a great excuse to pick up a bottle of Chambord, raspberry liqueur that comes in a sexy, globe-shaped gold-and-glass bottle. After all, when can you go wrong with raspberry?

1 ounce vodka
4 ounces champagne
½ ounce Chambord
1–2 fresh raspberries or 1 lime wedge, for garnish

Let that vodka flow into a chilled champagne flute, add the bubbly, then top with Chambord. Pop 1 or 2 fresh raspberries over the edge of the glass if you have some, otherwise lime wedges work just as well.

ONE OF THE MOST FAMOUS—AND PROBABLY THE SEXIEST—CHAMPIONS OF champagne was Marilyn Monroe, who, legend has it, bathed in more than 300 bottles of it! Try this at home—if you're a Rockefeller girl or a Vanderbilt chick, that is.

CHAMPAGNE COOLER

*V*ery elegant and even more refreshing. Cointreau's citrusy taste mixes so well with brandy's full-bodied flavor,
and champagne makes the whole thing crisp and cool. (If you
wish, go easy on the Cointreau, and add ½–1 ounce—like us,
you might not be a fan of ultra-orangey flavor.) But these ingredients don't come cheap, so save this special drink for a
momentous occasion.

1 ounce brandy
1 ounce Cointreau
3–4 ounces champagne
1 mint sprig, for garnish

In a cocktail shaker, pour brandy and Cointreau over ice.
Shake, shake, shake, and pour into a chilled champagne flute.
Then fill the glass to the brim with champagne, pop a mint
sprig on the side, and put the rest of the bottle on ice—if it
lasts that long!

Cherry Pop

We can't tell you exactly *why* Megan was inspired to dub this delicious drink the "Cherry Pop," but we'll say this much: It's got nothing to do with soda pop! But seriously, girls, the sweet and tart effect of the lemon vodka and grenadine gives a ton of attitude to its girly-pink color. This little treat goes over especially well at bachelorette parties!

1 ounce lemon vodka, chilled
4–5 ounces champagne
Dash of grenadine
1 maraschino cherry, for garnish

Watch the vodka glide into a chilled champagne flute, then fill 'er up with champagne. Add a dash or 2 of grenadine (or as much as you'd like) and float a cherry—or 2—on top. We like to save the cherry for last, but that's up to you . . .

THE FASHION INDUSTRY'S TOP MODELS LAUNCHED A CRAZE OF SIPPING CHAMpagne through a straw—so they didn't ruin their lipstick. Going a bit overboard? Perhaps, but it's sexier than smudges!

Mimosa Kiss

ou'll never have an awkward morning-after again when you know how to mix up a couple of these twisty takes on the traditional "orange juice–plus–champers" mimosa! When you need the hair of the dog that bit you—and if you're ready to jump-start his engine again—the gin-champagne combo is the perfect potion. Show him you're a master mixologist, then show off your other skills as you head back to bed for a "nap" . . .

2 ounces gin
2 ounces grapefruit juice
½ teaspoon maraschino cherry juice
Dash of Angostura bitters
3–4 ounces champagne
1 maraschino cherry, for garnish

Pour everything but the cherry into a blender over plenty of cracked ice. Pour into a chilled double Old-Fashioned glass. P.S., don't forget to add the cherry—it takes the edge off this cocktail's signature grapefruit taste.

Champagne Libre

The Cuba Libre is rum, lime, and cola. We're using champagne—and a few other variations—for an added punch. If you're throwing a south-of-the-border-type bash, this is the perfect prelude. Goes great with Latin-style appetizers, too, like hearts-of-palm and tomato salad, spicy calamari, or even a platter of nachos. Or serve it up as an after-dinner drink and get ready to rumba!

1½ ounces light rum
¼ ounce lime juice
½ teaspoon simple syrup (see page 58), or to taste
4–5 ounces champagne

Mix everything but the champagne in a cocktail shaker with cracked ice and strain into a chilled wine glass. Let the champagne flow till the glass is full or till the bottle is empty!

"Champagne is the only wine that leaves a woman beautiful after drinking." —Marquise de Pompadour, 18th-century diva

BUBBLY MOJITO

*M*ojito meets mint julep meets the bubbly in this hybrid of three of our favorite drinks. Mojitos are *the* drink of choice these days. Start your own trend by trying this take on them! Ernest Hemingway would be proud, and partygoers will be way impressed. Serve with finger foods like Manchego cheese and crackers, garlic-stuffed olives, or chunks of spicy chorizo.

6–7 fresh mint leaves
1 teaspoon simple syrup (see page 58)
½ ounce lime juice

2 ounces bourbon
4–5 ounces champagne
1 mint sprig, for garnish

Pop mint leaves into a tall Collins glass with simple syrup and muddle (see page 60). Slide ice cubes into the glass until it's two-thirds full, then add lime juice and bourbon and stir, stir, stir. Fill glass with ice-cold champagne, and stick a mint sprig over the rim of the glass. *Bonita!*

SEXY SAN FRANCISCO! DON'T MISS THE **BUBBLE LOUNGE**—714 MONT-gomery Street, (415) 434-4204—it's a champagne bar featuring more than 300 different types of bubbly. Great place to meet eligible financial types, too! Or get your date to take you to the View Lounge—at the top of the **Marriott Hotel**, 55 4th Street, (415) 442-6127—and sip flawless cocktails or champagne from 39 stories high. Another of our faves is **Pow!**—101 Sixth Street, (415) 278-0940—it will hit you right in the kisser with its funky superhero décor, naughty cartoons on the walls, and fun but dangerous cocktails. Try them all!

Black Velvet

Oh, your aching head. We know: we've been there. Sometimes there's nothing for it but this famous Irish cure for, well, for last night. And true to its name, it goes down so, so smoothly. You'd be surprised, but these are pretty strong! Take it easy, or you might be handing out your number to every Irishman in the bar before noon. (Is that a bad thing?)

½ part Guinness stout
½ part chilled champagne

Fill a Collins glass halfway with Guinness (no substitutions—other brands of stout don't make the cut!) then fill the rest with the champagne. Wait until the whole concoction settles—that is, it no longer looks cloudy—before you take the first delicious sip.

EVER WOKEN UP WITH SORE LEGS THE MORNING AFTER A LATE NIGHT, FEELING like you spent the evening at the gym instead of with a cocktail in your hand? No, it doesn't count as a workout; that muscle stiffness is due to dehydration. Just another reason to drink plenty of water before you go to bed and as soon as you wake up.

The Scarlett O'Hara

*F*rankly, my dear, you won't give a damn that Mr. Wrong just spilled his martini all over your favorite Jimmy Choos after one or two of these little gems! (Make sure he picks up your dry cleaning tab, though, and *not* your number—unless he's a regular Ashley, in which case, do take him home to Tara!) Talk about *southern comfort* . . .

1 slice orange or lemon peel
1 ounce Southern Comfort
Dash of Angostura bitters
3–4 ounces brut champagne

Twist an orange or lemon peel and give the rim of a chilled champagne flute a rubdown. Pour in the Southern Comfort, add bitters, and fill with champagne. Slip the orange or lemon peel over the side at a sexy angle, relax, and dream about your Rhett Butler.

SPLURGE ON THIS OUTRAGEOUS LITTLE NUMBER: A BOTTLE OF PIPER-HEIDSIECK champagne (now *that's* quality!) laced into a tight red mini-corset! Totally too hot to handle. Makes the best gift for your favorite champagne-o-phile.

CHAMPAGNE COSMOPOLITAN

Why settle for a cosmo plain, when it can have . . . champagne? Carrie, Samantha, Miranda, Charlotte, and friends would be proud of this elegant take on their favorite cocktail. Missed a few episodes? Rent the last couple of seasons, and sip a few of these while catching up. It's a great way to spend Thursday night when you just don't feel like a night on the town.

¼ ounce Grand Marnier
¼ ounce triple sec
2 ounces cranberry juice
1 splash lime juice
1 slice lime, for garnish
4 ounces champagne

Shake all ingredients except champagne over ice in a cocktail shaker. Strain into a cocktail glass and add champagne. Stir gently, and *voilà!*—a cosmo like you've never tasted before. Garnish with lime slice, then float a cranberry on top.

SPEAKING OF CORSETS, BUY ONE FOR YOURSELF WITH THAT YEAR-END BONUS! Top designers Stella and Chloe make gorgeous ones. Lace it up, admire your barely there waist, and sit back with a Champagne Cosmo in your hand.

$\mathscr{I}$t's true: If a little genie popped out of our beer bottle and said, "I'll grant you three drinks," we'd pick champagne first. Wouldn't you? After all, no other drink says "I am sleek, chic, and exceedingly cool" quite so gracefully. Whether you're having it straight up, or in the form of a Bellini or a Raspberry Risqué, it's delicious, refreshing, and adds a touch of class to any evening. Did we mention it makes a great gift, too? Bring a bottle to a housewarming or birthday party, and you'll get more gratitude than you can handle in your thank-you card.

CHAPTER 3

Retro-Cool

What's old is always new! Sometimes it's just plain fun to trash trendy drinks for a night, and go retro. From the Roaring Twenties to Disco Fever, drinks of decades past are making a comeback. From the Sidecar to the Golden Cadillac, these quirky concoctions are taking on whole new lives. And we've given you the best of them here!

Before you head out to Polly Esther's for 1970s-style fun, or dash out to swing dance with your beau, whip up a few of these libations from long ago to put you in the mood. Most of them are as simple as one or two great liqueurs or spirits combined flawlessly. Have the girls over for Mai Tais, or serve a Rob Roy to your favorite boy. A couple of minor liquor cabinet investments should get you rolling.

What *is* a Pink Squirrel? A Brandy Alexander? A Pink Lady? These aren't just names on placemats anymore. They're delicious and—best of all—they're all right here.

Shirley Temple and the Devil

*T*his Shirley grew up to be just a little bit wicked—like we did. Who'd have thought this spiked version of your childhood favorite could be such a kitschy-yet-cool party drink? And the best thing is, you can drink them all night long— they're delicious, but not strong enough to make you see stars the next morning.

1½ ounces whiskey
4 ounces ginger ale
1 teaspoon grenadine
1 orange slice
1 maraschino cherry

Toss the whiskey, then ginger ale, then grenadine into an Old-Fashioned glass over plenty of ice. Nothing more to it! Except don't forget to add the orange slice and cherry—just for fun! (We like to make an oversized version of this drink and serve it in a pint glass. Just double the recipe and say the devil made you do it.)

"Let there be dancing in the streets, drinking in the saloons, and necking in the opera."
—Groucho Marx as Otis B. Driftwood, in the movie *A Night at the Opera*

Pink Lady

This pale pink cocktail smacks of 1940s-style elegance. The traditional recipe calls for egg whites, which can be tricky—we decided to give them the boot. (Who needs complications?) Nonetheless, it's a smooth way for you and your ladies to kick off any evening. Speaking of 1940s chic, try swing dancing after a few Pink Ladies have put you in the mood! Some swing clubs even offer free lessons—and they're a great place to meet eligible bachelors.

1½ ounces gin
1½ ounces applejack brandy
1 ounce lemon juice
1 teaspoon simple syrup (see page 58)
1 teaspoon grenadine

Everything gets tossed over ice—even the grenadine—in a cocktail shaker. Have chilled cocktail glasses on hand; after you shake it up, strain it gently into one of them. Repeat, repeat, repeat. They'll be in high demand all night!

GIMLET

What's a Gimlet? We'll fill you in. You've probably heard of it, but did you know it's the new Gin and Tonic? To be specific, it's the booze of your choice combined with fresh lime juice. It's been around awhile, but it's re-emerging as a great alternative to G&Ts or even martinis. The traditional Gimlet features gin; try it with Tanqueray or Bombay Sapphire for best results.

2 ounces gin
½ ounce fresh lime juice
1 lime peel

Mix all ingredients except lime peel vigorously in a mixing glass and pour into a chilled Old-Fashioned glass. Twist lime peel over rim, and you're done in an instant. (P.S. Don't spend hours squeezing limes. Fresh lime juice is available at any grocery store. We found this out the hard way!)

ARE YOU A "CLASSY BROAD"? OF COURSE YOU ARE! THE LADIES OF LUPEC are like-minded gals. Ladies United for the Preservation of Endangered Cocktails are the Retro Drink Police. They're dedicated to making sure drinks from days gone by don't become extinct. Check out their fab recipes, tips, reviews, and more at www.lupec.org. You might even want to start a chapter in your city!

Rob Roy

This one's been a classic for practically forever. (Okay, at least since the 1920s, when your Rob Roy was a dime, and you got a free lunch of salty bar snacks while you were at it.) Watch out: There's nothing syrupy-sweet about this retro tough-girl—or tough-guy—drink. Serve 'em up with meaty-but-classy snacks such as cocktail franks, smoked oysters on crackers, or pâté on rye.

2 ounces Scotch
½ ounce sweet vermouth
Dash of orange bitters
1 maraschino cherry

Pour all ingredients except the cherry into a mixing glass along with several ice cubes. Stir well. (Don't shake this time!) Strain into a chilled cocktail glass. Pop that cherry on top, sit back, and sip.

"Jane was not sure how drunk she was, and could not bring herself to stand up, this being the test."
—Muriel Spark, from her novel, *The Girls of Slender Means*

BRANDY ALEXANDER

*Y*ou didn't think brandy and chocolate could work wonders together? What about those chocolate mini liqueur bottles you love nibbling at the holidays? It's true, chocolate and cordials are a heavenly combination. Sip one after relaxing over coffee to make the night last longer. Your date won't be able to say no to these sweet and creamy treats.

1½ ounces brandy
1 ounce crème de cacao
1 ounce heavy cream

Mix all ingredients with cracked ice in a shaker or blender and strain into a chilled cocktail glass. Perfect for a post-date rendezvous at your place—it's such fun to swirl each rich sip over your tongue . . . or over each other's!

IT'S A SNAP TO MAKE "STRIPED" OR LAYERED COCKTAILS WITH CORDIALS LIKE THE brandy and crème de cacao in the Brandy Alexander. (Try the Chocolate Cherry Kiss on page 97.) Pour each ingredient over a spoon (bottom-side up) into the glass, and make sure you do so in the order in which the recipe specifies. The result? A layered libation that's almost too pretty to drink—although we're sure that won't stop you!

OLD-FASHIONED

This drink is as simple as they come. You'll want to use the best bourbon you can find, not the happy-hour-quality stuff! Believe us, you'll taste the difference, since bourbon's in the spotlight here, and the other ingredients are just the trimmings. This anti-girly drink is a cocktail-hour staple. Add some savory, old-school munchies like a bowl of cashews, sharp Cheddar cheese and crackers, or mini spinach quiches, and get a rep as the classiest hostess around.

> 2 ounces bourbon (or rye)
> Dash of water
> Dash of simple syrup (see page 58), to taste
> Dash of Angostura bitters

Mix everything in a cocktail glass; then add a few ice cubes. Stir it gently and you're all set. If you've got a gentleman caller, you might not want to spend too much time playing bartender, anyway!

SIDECAR

$\mathcal{I}$t was in high fashion in the 1920s, along with flappers, long strings of beads, and the Charleston. Now it's back, being spotted in many swank cocktail spots. And the best part? You can whip one up in hardly more than a second. Forgo the bar snacks when you're sipping these and get in the spirit of the 1920s, when a liquid lunch was the style of the moment.

1½ ounces brandy
¾ ounce curaçao or Cointreau
½ ounce lemon juice

Mix all ingredients with cracked ice in a shaker and strain into that well-chilled cocktail glass you always have on hand. Put some Josephine Baker on the gramophone, and be glad Prohibition's a thing of the past!

THE SIDECAR WAS THE HOTTEST DRINK IN TOWN IN THE ROARING TWENTIES; now it's making an elegant comeback. Pair it with a little black dress by Diane von Furstenberg—the statement you'll make is simple, sexy chic.

French Kiss

*I*t's the best kind there is! Both types of vermouth mixed in perfect equilibrium. Isn't that what a kiss is supposed to be?

1 ounce sweet vermouth   1 ounce dry vermouth

Swirl both kinds of vermouth over ice in a cocktail glass and stir. No garnish needed—all you have to do is pucker up!

Manhattan

*I*s it as good as the city that gave it its name? We think so! (Thanks, NYC.) A great break from those too-sweet drinks that it's easy to get addicted to. When you want something that's more crisp than it is sticky or sugary, try one of these. We like them with anything salty. They're a great excuse to nibble pretzels, salt and vinegar potato chips, or dry-roasted peanuts.

1½ ounces rye whiskey   Dash of Angostura bitters
¼ ounce sweet vermouth   1 maraschino cherry

Swirl everything but the cherry over ice in a mixing glass, stir gently, and strain into chilled cocktail glass. (A shortcut: If your cocktail shaker's MIA, you can easily mix this drink right in the glass.) Don't forget the cherry—we sometimes like to add 2 or 3, just for fun.

GIBSON

Be a Gibson girl! Our only advice for this little libation: Make sure you have gum or mints on hand, because if you like to nibble the cocktail onion after you finish your drink, you're going to need to freshen your breath! Or, if your breath's less than minty, just make sure your date has a mint, too, and he'll never notice a thing. Best bets for appetizers: a bowl of olives, a plate of cheese sticks, or hardboiled eggs.

2½ ounces gin
Few dashes of dry vermouth
2–3 cocktail onions, for garnish

Pour gin into that all-important mixing glass over ice cubes. Add the dashes of dry vermouth with care. (You don't want to overdo the vermouth in this one!) Stir briskly and strain into a chilled cocktail glass. Pop a couple of pearly-white cocktail onions over the edge for a finishing touch.

IF YOUR TUMMY'S IN A TIZZY FROM LAST NIGHT'S FABULOUS GOOD TIMES, nibble on some fresh ginger. Or try pickled ginger, which comes free with takeout sushi. (So remember the next time you order out: Instead of tossing it, tuck it away in the fridge for emergencies!) Crystallized ginger works wonderfully, too. Hangover, begone!

Golden Cadillac

S how off those bellbottoms and platforms while you're sipping this far-out disco drink! Just ask Travolta how great they are (but don't say we sent you). Plus, Galliano's tall, slim, tapered bottle itself drips elegance, as does its enchanting greeny-gold color. Try it to cool off (or to ignite!) your Saturday night fever, as guests arrive at your disco inferno. (No quaaludes, please—your 1970s-style shindig doesn't need to be *that* authentic.)

1 ounce Galliano
1 ounce white crème de cacao
1 ounce cream
2–3 cocoa beans, for garnish

Pour all ingredients over ice into shaker. Strain into an Old-Fashioned glass. Garnish with cocoa beans, and your man will be begging you to drive his car, baby.

"First you take a drink,
then the drink takes a drink,
then the drink takes you."
—F. Scott Fitzgerald

HARVEY WALLBANGER

Bang *what*? Who's Harvey? It's a mystery to us, too, but rest assured that this ain't your average screwdriver. Great before a night out, and it makes a nice morning-after drink (after you've stopped wall-banging yourself). Try it at brunch with bacon and eggs or a cheesy omelet for energy after a wild night (along with that much-needed cup of coffee, of course).

1½–2 ounces vodka
4 ounces orange juice
½ ounce Galliano

Let the vodka flow! Into a chilled glass with a few ice cubes, that is! Add the orange juice and stir well, then pool the Galliano on top. We guarantee it'll ring your bell.

THE WINDY CITY IS HOME TO HOT PLACES LIKE **LE COLONIAL**—937 NORTH Rush Street, (312) 255-0088—which features cigars, swanky food, and haute couture libations. (Did we hear something about a marvelous Mango Margarita? For our recipe, see page 57.) Then there's **Nine Steak House**—440 West Randolph Street, (312) 277-0207—which features a champagne bar that's *crème de la crème*, and sleek, stylin' décor. If you want to kick back over massive margaritas at a slightly more casual joint, try **Lalo's**—500 N. LaSalle Street, (312) 329-0030—and don't miss their good Mexican fare.

STINGER

The Stinger is nothing less than inspiring. You'll certainly feel good after a few sips of this smooth, strong libation. The richness of both brandy and crème de menthe make this a better digestif than aperitif, if dinner's on the agenda; if not, sip them at the beginning of the evening, so you can enjoy them.

1½ ounces brandy   1½ ounces white crème de menthe
mint sprig, for garnish

Just mix both ingredients with cracked ice in a shaker or blender and pour the chilly mix into an equally chilly cocktail glass. Slip a mint sprig over the side, and you're done!

FRENCH CONNECTION

And you thought it was just a place to shop! Before you were spending all your money on cute T-shirts from the store of the same name, hipsters were kicking these back while boogying and playing funky music. Break out your K.C. and the Sunshine Band records, and pour one (or two, or three) of these!

1½ ounces cognac   1 orange slice, for garnish
1 ounce amaretto

Swirl the cognac, then the amaretto, over ice cubes in a chilled Old-Fashioned glass. Add an orange slice for garnish, then get out your grooviest accessories and get down!

MAI TAI

"Bring me another Mai Tai!" You've seen them on those menus in Chinese restaurants, but have you ever tried one? (We took the plunge and were rewarded with a huge drink in a ceramic pineapple. No kidding!) So kitschy they're cool, Mai Tais are sweet, rummy, fruity, funky concoctions. Oh, and the color—bright blue—is great, too. Ceramic pineapple optional.

1 ounce light rum
1 ounce dark rum
½ ounce blue curaçao
Juice of 1 lime
¼ ounce simple syrup (see page 58)
1 lime peel, for garnish
1 orange peel, for garnish

You'll get the party started right by mixing everything except the lime and orange peels in a cocktail shaker or blender (use a blender if you're doubling or tripling this recipe). Pour into a chilled glass, and twist those citrus peels at cocky little angles over the rim—a masterpiece of mixology.

LEGEND HAS IT THAT MAI TAI MEANS "OUT OF THIS WORLD" IN TAHITIAN. Don't ask how we know, but keep it in mind for your next tropical vacation!

Windjammer

$\mathcal{I}$t's a distant relative of the piña colada, with a few little extras like cream, spice, and a hint of chocolate. We don't know why this isn't in every bar and restaurant around town; it's pure indulgence over ice. Skip the standard frozen drinks at your next shindig, and surprise everyone with a few of these. Tropical fruit, like mangoes, papayas, melon, and pineapple—or other light, sweet snacks—are a Windjammer's best friends.

1½ ounces Jamaica rum
1½ ounces light rum
1½ ounces white crème de cacao
6 ounces pineapple juice
1 ounce heavy cream
Sprinkle of grated nutmeg, for garnish
1 pineapple slice, for garnish

Booze, juice, and cream all get tossed over cracked ice in a cocktail shaker. Shake well—until the cocktail shaker is frothy—and pour into an Old-Fashioned glass. Sprinkle with grated nutmeg (you might want to experiment with other spices like cinnamon or cloves, too) and add a slice of pineapple for a tropical touch.

ou've heard jaded folks declare, "There's nothing new under the sun." We agree, but add, "and that's great!" The ghosts of drinks past are continually making comebacks from relative obscurity. (There was actually a time when martinis were considered stuffy and been-done instead of classy and fun, believe it or not!) What's next? Maybe it's the Gimlet, which has already been spotted in a few joints here and there; the same goes for the sexy Sidecar. Or maybe a good old-fashioned Old-Fashioned is due for another dose of limelight. Try them all, then decide for yourself!

CHAPTER 4

SULTRY SIPPING: DRINKS THAT CHILL

*I*t's summer in the city, your apartment is sweltering, and a walk down the street is even worse. No sweat! Bring out your barely-there bikinis and whip up a few of these frosty, frothy drinks, then lounge on the roof all afternoon.

Or make enough to share! No air conditioning in your apartment, and no penthouse swimming pool? Keep your city beach party cool by tripling or quadrupling these recipes. All you need is a blender and a dream. It's easy to transform any too-toasty fifth-floor walkup into a tropical paradise in no time flat.

Or, you could shoo out your friends and just invite a date over for drinks for two. When things get too hot to handle—and they will—keep a couple of Creamsicles or Mango Margaritas on hand in the fridge to heat things up even more. Hope your bedroom's air-conditioned!

From the kitschy Piña Colada, to the mellow Mojito, and the dreamy Creamsicle, the drinks in this chapter can't help but keep you chill, in winter and summer alike. Cheers!

Mojito

The Mojito is the trendiest thing to hit summer since—well, bathing suits. Whatever. It's the drink of the moment! You've had them at your favorite cocktail spot, so you know the tangy, fruity flavors of mint and lime offset the rum so well. Now you can try them yourself—you mistress of mixology, you deserve to show off your skills at that cocktail party you're having in July. *Olé!*

½ lime
1 tablespoon sugar
Several sprigs of mint
2 ounces light rum
Dash of club soda or dark rum

Squeeze the juice of the lime into a chilled double Old-Fashioned glass. Add the sugar and mint, and muddle until the sugar's dissolved and you can smell the mint's fragrance. Fill the glass with crushed ice and add the light rum. Swizzle until the glass turns frosty. Top off with either club soda or—our preference—dark rum.

IT'S TRUE, THE MOJITO WAS ERNEST HEMINGWAY'S FAVORITE DRINK—BEFORE it became *the* choice for sipping on sultry August afternoons. (It lifts our spirits much more than *The Old Man and the Sea* or *For Whom the Bell Tolls*.)

Caipirinha

*A*h, Cachaca. A couple years ago, no one could even spell it; now, it's everywhere from sleek-and-chic establishments to the divey little bar around the corner. If you haven't had a Caipirinha during a night on the town, find a great Brazilian restaurant or bar and taste what you've been missing. (Do so with caution, though! The Caipirinha has been known to challenge even those of us with exceptionally high tolerance.)

2 ounces Cachaca (a rum-like Brazilian spirit made from sugar cane)
½ ounce fresh lime juice
1 tablespoon sugar
Rind of ¼ lime, cut into strips (save the juice of those limes for the margaritas later in this chapter!)

Cachaca, lime juice, sugar, and yes, even the lime rinds all get thrown into the mix over ice in a cocktail shaker. Then (surprise, surprise) shake. Strain into a chilled Old-Fashioned glass, on the rocks. Hint: This drink has been known to give imbibers the munchies. Have Brazilian appetizers on hand, such as hearts of palm salad, or chunks of chorizo sausage.

CACHACA IS THE NEWEST CRAZE—IT'S MADE FROM SUGAR CANE JUICE, BUT BY itself tastes absolutely terrible. Always, always mix it with something fun; try honey, sugar, and/or lime, lemon, or orange juices. Sheree and Megan deny all responsibility for clothes ruined by spitting out spirits!

Pacific Rim Cocktail

*T*here's nothing like ice-cold vodka to turn a sweltering evening into a midsummer night's dream. This martini-like concoction features ginger liqueur, giving it an Asian-esque flavor. You might also substitute chilled sake (Japanese rice wine) for vodka to give the drink an even more authentically Asian taste. Mix up a batch for a sushi party! Either order takeout, or try making it yourself with fresh veggies, cooked crabmeat, avocado, or shrimp tempura.

3–4 ounces iced vodka (or sake)
½ ounce ginger liqueur (at room temperature)

If vodka is not ice cold, pour it into a cocktail shaker over ice and shake well. Strain into a chilled martini glass. Then, carefully add the ginger liqueur; it'll trickle down to the bottom of the glass, then fountain back up to the top of the drink. If you want to impress a date with your spirits savvy, this is the drink to choose!

Piña Colada

Come on, who doesn't like Piña Coladas? You'd think the P.C. would become cliché at some point, and perhaps it has, but that doesn't stop anyone from loving the pineapple-coconut combination. Want to make a virgin version? Go ahead; this drink is so yummy, you won't even miss the alcohol. Don't go overboard on the coconut juice, though—its sweetness can over-power the rum (and you wouldn't want to do that, would you?).

2 ounces gold rum
2 ounces cream of coconut
4 ounces pineapple juice

1 maraschino cherry, for garnish
1 lime wedge, for garnish
1 pineapple wedge, for garnish

Mix all ingredients—except the garnishes—with cracked ice in a cocktail shaker. Pour into a chilled Collins glass. Pop a cherry—the *maraschino* kind, girls—into it, and try drizzling the cherry liquid into it, too, for a sweet, swirly effect. Rim with lime and pineapple wedges, or with just about any fruit you can think of.

GOT DARK CIRCLES UNDER YOUR EYES THIS MORNING—AGAIN? NO ONE AT the office will ever know if you cover them up with yellow concealer. Yellow neutralizes those dark blue, telltale signs of a late night and a few cocktails. Before you apply foundation, dot your undereye circles with concealer, then blend carefully. Add foundation and blush or skin highlighter, and you'll look like you slept like a baby.

MARGARITA, UP

¡Tequila! The margarita is a year-round favorite, but everyone seems to suck them down like water as soon as the weather gets hot. There are tons of fun variations, but here's the classic recipe that no party girl can do without. (Try making margaritas in oversized glasses; then hollow out lime halves, fill them with tequila, and float them on top for an elegant, potent potable.)

3 ounces white or gold tequila	Juice of 1 large lime
1 ounce triple sec	Coarse salt, to rim glass (optional)

Swirl tequila, triple sec, and lime juice into a cocktail shaker over cracked ice. Rub the rim of a chilled cocktail glass with a lime wedge and dip the rim of the glass in a saucer of coarse salt until it's as salty as you like it. After a few bicep-toning shakes (who knew you were working out while making cocktails?), just strain it into a glass. Put on some salsa or merengue, and let the games begin!

THE AGAVE PLANT, FROM WHICH TEQUILA IS MADE, WAS REVERED BY ANCIENT Mexicans as a holy plant—it symbolized the goddess Mayaheul, who had 400 breasts. Wow. We're not sure what Mayaheul was protectress of, but we're pretty certain she wasn't the goddess of step aerobics. Ouch!

Mango Margarita, Up

Tequila is really Mexico's vodka—it goes with just about anything. And fruit, especially tropical fruit, is one of the best accompaniments. (Hey, it's nutritious, to boot!) Plus, this is such a pretty drink; the orangey shade is bound to lift your spirits and add an edge to your next backyard bash. Keep it simple, and just serve with baskets of chips and salsa, or go all out with quesadillas, nachos, and a spicy, southern-style salad.

3 ounces triple sec
¾ ounce lime juice
3 mango pieces
1 ounce of tequila

Pour triple sec and lime juice into a mixing glass. (No ice yet!) Then add the mango, and muddle well. Add the tequila and ice, shake well, and strain into a chilled salted cocktail glass. Not a salt maven? Rim the glass with sugar instead. Either way, it's a mango masterpiece.

THE FUNKY ORANGE COLOR OF A MANGO MARGARITA HAS GOT TO MATCH something by Betsey Johnson! No one does beads, lace, and wild colors like she does. Find the nearest Betsey boutique, and step into something fun for those nights of summer lovin'.

THE HAMPTONS

It's an instant vacation! If you can't get away from the sultry city during those dog days, never fear, you'll feel like you're steps away from the beach with this taste of the tropics. Even the fresh green color is rejuvenating. Skip the time-share and head straight for the blender! Then spend the cash you save on a new bikini. (Now *that's* financial planning!)

1½ ounces vodka
3½ ounces pineapple juice
Juice of 1 lime
½ teaspoon simple syrup (see below for recipe)
½ ounce green crème de menthe
1 pineapple slice, for garnish
1 lime slice, for garnish

Toss everything but the crème de menthe and the fruit into a cocktail shaker or blender with cracked ice. Pour into a hurricane glass, add the crème de menthe, and slip the fruit slices over the rim . . . then just sail away from it all.

SINCE SUGAR CRYSTALS DON'T DISSOLVE WELL IN ALCOHOL, SIMPLE SYRUP IS essential to have on hand for sweetening summer drinks. It's easy to make: just mix 1 cup of water with 1 cup of sugar (use more or less sugar depending on the desired sweetness and thickness) and boil it for 5 minutes. It'll stay fresh practically forever in the fridge.

Strawberry Liplicker

$\mathcal{G}$t wouldn't be summer without a drink featuring the smooth, coconut-tinged flavor of Malibu! And with fresh berries and a touch of vodka, your friends will be asking for this luscious libation long after Labor Day. Try it with fresh raspberries instead of strawberries, or use both. Have an indoor picnic with a batch of Liplickers, fun sandwiches (try fresh mozzarella and tomato, or spicy chicken and avocado), and fruit and brownies for dessert.

1 ounce vodka
2 ounces Malibu rum
¼ cup fresh strawberries, sliced
Whole strawberries, for garnish

Mix everything except the whole berries in a blender with cracked ice and blend until silky smooth. Pour into a chilled wine glass, and garnish with a whole. Everyone'll be licking their glasses clean.

Frozen Mint Julep

Today, Kentucky; tomorrow, the world! This frozen version of everyone's favorite Derby Day drink isn't just for a day in May—it'll keep any summertime gathering cool. Place bets on how many times you'll be going back to the blender for more—we bet it'll be in the triple digits. It's just the thing for your next barbeque.

2 ounces bourbon
1 ounce lemon juice
1 ounce simple syrup (see page 58)
6 mint leaves
1 mint sprig, for garnish

Muddle the bourbon, lemon juice, simple syrup, and mint in any old glass. Toss it into a blender with the mint leaves and plenty of crushed ice and blend until almost smooth. Serve in a cocktail glass and slide a mint sprig on the edge of the glass.

IN A MUDDLE ABOUT MUDDLING? NO FEAR, IT'S BASICALLY A SYNONYM FOR "mush well." You can use the handle of a wooden spoon, or, if you want to go all out, you can actually buy a muddler just about anywhere barware is sold. Use the spoon or muddler to crush the lime, mint, sugar, or other ingredients, in the glass. This releases the yummy essences of each flavor.

CREAMSICLE

*M*egan created this little concoction at her favorite bar when she was in the mood for something cold and creamy, light and refreshing, and icy and edgy. The result? A drinkable dessert that tastes as great as those famous frozen treats you had when you were a kid. Substitute 2 ounces of raspberry vodka for an extra twist.

4 ounces vanilla vodka   ¾–1 cup whole milk
1 ounce Cointreau

Combine all ingredients in a blender with plenty of ice. Blend on high until frothy and smooth. (This serves 1, but you might want to share with a buddy or a date—it's pretty potent!)

Oh, no: You've had more than a few vodka tonics at that company party, and now you're trying desperately to pretend you're just fine. But how?

- Sit down! Don't stand up unless you have to.
- Drink water and/or cola—you need nonalcoholic beverages, and a small dose of caffeine can't hurt.
- Eat! Forget calories for the moment. A mix of carbs and protein is best, like cheese nachos, mini pizzas, or grilled chicken skewers with pita.
- Whatever you do, don't approach your boss! Hang out with a couple of trusted coworkers instead.
- Once you've lost that wobbly feeling, get up and dance! The movement will help get rid of the effects of the alcohol.

CRÈME DE MENTHE CRUSH

Remember Slurpees? Well, you won't find this one at the corner convenience store! This mix of ice and pure mintyness is the best kind of refreshment when the temperature soars. Plus, it's a snap to make, with just two ingredients you probably have on hand already. If you're tired of frozen margaritas but are in the mood for something equally chill, you'll thrill to a couple of these.

3 ounces crème de menthe
1 mint sprig

Fill a chilled cocktail glass with plenty of finely crushed ice (use a blender and blend on high until ice chunks are small and almost grainy). Add green crème de menthe, and stir well. Serve it up with cocktail straws, or for a funky touch, clip some regular striped drinking straws in half and add a jaunty little mint sprig. P.S. This drink comes with an added bonus: You can skip the breath mints!

PASSION FRUIT DAIQUIRI

*F*ind out why it's called "passion" fruit—it won't take you long once you dive into one of these! This isn't the daiquiri your parents were drinking back in the 1970s; it's an icy, exotic mix of tropical fruit and rum that's sailing right into the 21st century. Been invited to a BYOB party? Bring the ingredients for this drink, and no one will touch the light beer and cheap whiskey that less-creative partygoers brought.

1½ ounces light rum
½ ounce lime juice
½ ounce simple syrup (see page 58)
½ ounce passion fruit juice

Mix all ingredients with cracked ice in a shaker or blender and strain into a chilled cocktail glass.

So you're going out, and you just know it's going to be a late night. One caveat to keep in mind when you get dressed: Never, and we mean never, wear your good jewelry! More than one favorite piece of ours has been lost in sink drains, flung irretrievably into the corners of restaurants, and torn from around necks and wrists. Wear the cheap stuff—you'll still look great!

Sangria

There are so many recipes for Sangria ("blood" in Spanish), but this one is the simplest you'll see anywhere. If you're called upon to bring booze to a party, don't bring cheap vodka or a plain old bottle of wine. Show up with sangria—and maybe some tapas, or finger foods, like mini burritos or bacon-wrapped shrimp—and your host will thank you again and again.

4 bottles dry red wine	3 oranges
1 cup brandy, or less to taste	3 apples
3 lemons	3 limes

Slice fruit in any combination you'd like—feel free to adjust the amount of fruit you use—and place in a 1-gallon pitcher. Pour brandy and wine over fruit and pop into the fridge for a few hours, to let the flavors mingle. Stir, and serve over lots of ice.

BOSTON'S NOT JUST FOR PILGRIMS ANYMORE! IT'S HOME TO LOADS OF HOT bars and clubs. Try **Sophia's**—1270 Boylston Street, (617) 351-7001—for a night of salsa dancing and free-flowing Sangria. Or for classy, after-work drinks, like special martinis and other great cocktails, splurge on an evening at the **Oak Bar**—138 Saint James Avenue (617) 267-5300. If your date is a hep cat, treat him to jazz at **Scullers Jazz Club**—400 Soldiers Field Road (Allston), (617) 562-4131—Boston's best jazz club, and sip smooth wines and cocktails while enjoying even smoother jazz.

Raspberry Cooler

uys and girls alike were asking for this cran-fruity cooler all night at one of the best bars around, the laid-back, low-key Dead Poet in NYC. Why? Because it's thirst-quenchingly cold, it's just sweet enough, and the vodka–triple sec combo adds a nice little bite. But don't take our word for it. Try it yourself!

2 ounces raspberry vodka
1 ounce triple sec
4 ounces cranberry juice
Splash of lemon-lime soda

In a mixing glass over lots of ice, swirl the vodka, triple sec, and cranberry juice together. Shake it up; add a splash of lemon-lime soda on top. Even if you're on the wagon, skip your usual cranberry and seltzer this once—you'll hardly know the difference!

"Drink to me."
—Pablo Picasso's last words

It's August, and you're greeting all your friends with, "It's so *hot*!" instead of, "Hi." Especially in the city, summer can be super-stifling, and sometimes it feels like there's just no way to relax. We know; we've been there. That's why we dedicated this entire chapter to cocktails that'll refresh both body and spirit. You've finally learned how to make a Mojito, and you've fallen head over heels for the Strawberry Liplicker. Now do it yourself! All you need is the booze of your choice, ice, a blender, and a little inspiration. There's no better way to beat the heat.

CHAPTER 5

THE HOTTEST DRINKS
FOR THE COLDEST NIGHTS

*P*icture this: The sun's about to set and you jump on the chairlift for one last run down your favorite slope. Your ears are tingling, your toes are numb even though they're buckled inside ski boots, and you haven't been able to feel your fingers since lunchtime. You're feeling like an Arctic penguin, not a ski bunny—and you'd give your right arm for a hot drink—if it weren't frostbitten, that is.

Or maybe you're running around the city on December 23, desperately searching for last-minute holiday presents among steady, icy snow and snarling shoppers. Your feet are sore, your new boots are soaked, *and* you still need gifts for Mom, Aunt Barbara, and your *boss!* Bah, humbug!

Well, it's time to come in from the cold and curl up by a roaring fire (or a radiator!) and relax with a steamy drink. Whether you're mixing them up for a date or a festive holiday party, these drinks are sure to warm you. From whipped-creamy Irish Coffee to Hot Toddies, and from homemade Hottest Hot Chocolate to the Café Royale, they are drinks for all seasons.

Irish Coffee

*L*eave it to the Irish to come up with one of the most popular coffee drinks of all time! Don't wait till St. Patrick's Day—invest in some good Irish whiskey, and serve this after your next dinner party. Try it with crunchy biscotti for a combination that spans, well, nations. *Slainte!*

2 teaspoons brown sugar
1 cup of hot coffee

1½–2 ounces Irish whiskey
1–2 tablespoons whipped cream

Rinse a glass coffee mug with hot water. Add the sugar and coffee. Stir until sugar is dissolved. Add whiskey, and top with lots of luscious whipped cream. Now you know why Irish eyes are smiling!

Cape Cod in Winter

*T*he Cape Codder is a staple of any party. But have you tried it hot? Heat up your next shindig with a few batches of this wonderful winter warmer.

1 cup cranberry juice
2 ounces vodka
1 cinnamon stick

1 lemon peel
¼ teaspoon ground cloves

Warm everything except the cloves in a saucepan—let it simmer, but don't let it boil. Pour into a warm mug and sprinkle the ground cloves on top. Use a fresh cinnamon stick to stir, and slide a fresh lemon twist over the side of the mug. Marvelous!

GLUHWEIN

When Megan ordered a cup of this "glowing wine" on a warm June evening in Konstanz, Germany, the bartender eyed her oddly. Who knew it was mainly a Christmas treat? But it's delicious any time of the year. Don't let the idea of warm wine scare you—it's a spicy, fruity concoction that's akin to hot cider. Try mixing in raisins and nuts; they're a nice surprise to find at the bottom of your glass when it's empty.

6 ounces dry red wine
1 cinnamon stick, broken into pieces
$\frac{1}{8}$ tablespoon ground nutmeg
2–3 fresh cloves or $\frac{1}{8}$ teaspoon ground cloves
2 teaspoons honey, or more to taste
1 whole cinnamon stick, optional
1 lemon peel, optional
1 orange peel, optional

This drink takes the prize for Fewest Dishes to Wash after Making. Just heat everything over a low flame in a pan until the honey is fully dissolved. Serve in a glass coffee mug and pop in a whole cinnamon stick or lemon and orange peels for garnish. *Prost!*

"In vino veritas." ("In wine there is truth.") —Pliny the Elder
He was right, wasn't he?

Hot Toddy

Can booze actually be good for you? Sure! When Megan had a cold while traveling in Ireland, a well-meaning local approached her in a café and told her if she hadn't had a hot toddy, she needed one! It's true—a hot toddy is just the remedy for a scratchy throat or a stubborn cold. If your sweetie's feeling under the weather, offer to pop up to his pad and mix one up for him. Doctor's orders have never tasted so good.

2 ounces whiskey
1–2 teaspoons sugar
2 lemon slices, for garnish
1 orange slice, for garnish
3–4 whole cloves, for garnish

Rinse a ceramic mug or glass coffee mug with hot water; then add whiskey, sugar, and 1 lemon slice and fill with hot (but not boiling!) water. Stir and slip lemon and orange slices over the edge of the mug. (A little vitamin C never hurts, especially if you're not feeling so hot.) Float the cloves on top.

"A torchlight procession marching down your throat."
—John L. O'Sullivan, on whiskey

Hottest Hot Chocolate

You loved it when you were a kid, and you're still addicted now—with good reason! But skip the powdered mix for once, grab a saucepan (don't worry, you're not actually cooking!), and mix up the ultimate comfort drink. Hot chocolate is great straight up, of course, and it's also heavenly with all sorts of liqueurs. Try Irish cream, white crème de menthe, Frangelico, or Kahlua.

1 tablespoon unsweetened cocoa
2 teaspoons sugar, or more to taste
¾–1 cup milk
1 ounce Irish cream or white crème de menthe

Stir the cocoa and sugar in a saucepan. Add the milk (pouring slowly) and heat over a medium flame until hot, but not boiling! Remove from heat, pour 1 ounce Irish cream or white crème de menthe (or whatever your favorite liqueur might be) into a large mug, and swirl the hot chocolate right over it. Now curl up on the couch, pop in a DVD, and relax . . . or make it for the perfect ending to a quiet night at home with your honey.

Hot Buttered Rum

Okay, so it might cost you a few more minutes on the Stairmaster tomorrow morning. But that's no reason not to try this tummy-warming classic! It's just the thing to take the chill away from a cold December night. Invite the girls over, whip up a batch of sugar cookies, and indulge in a comfort-food fest.

1 tablespoon sugar
2 cinnamon sticks
1 lemon peel
6 ounces hot water
3 ounces dark rum

1 pat of butter
1 sprinkle of cinnamon, for garnish
1 sprinkle of nutmeg, for garnish
1 sprinkle of cloves, for garnish

Rinse a glass coffee mug with hot water and add the sugar, 1 cinnamon stick, and lemon peel. Add the hot water and stir until the sugar is completely dissolved. Pour in the rum and stir again. Drop the pat of butter on top, sprinkle with spices (like cinnamon, nutmeg, or cloves) and serve with another cinnamon stick (it's fun to use them as stirrers).

PHILLY IS PACKED WITH HAPPENING PLACES LIKE **GLAM**—52 SOUTH 2ND STREET, (267) 671-0840—which features a dance floor downstairs and a seductive, couch-laden VIP lounge upstairs (where everyone's a VIP). Don't miss **Nile**—120 Chestnut Street, (215) 925-2363—a fun Middle Eastern joint with yummy cocktails and a belly dancer to boot! Then there's dark, smoky, divey-cool **Silk City Diner**—435 Spring Garden Street, (215) 592-8838—where you can relax with a cocktail at the dimly lit bar, or dance to the tunes of Philly's best DJs.

WARM APPLE CIDER

Nothing suits a crisp autumn evening better than Warm Apple Cider! When the mercury drops, this ultra-easy warm-me-up drink is the best way to stay toasty. Its sweet spiciness makes it the perfect complement to fall treats such as gingerbread cookies, snickerdoodles, and pumpkin pie. Don't be deceived by its deceptively smooth delivery—try not to have one too many or you'll wake up with a holiday headache the next morning, guaranteed.

6 ounces apple cider (whatever you do, don't substitute apple juice!)
Cinnamon, to rim glass
1½ ounces dark rum
1 cinnamon stick, for garnish
1 thin orange slice, for garnish
Dash of cloves
Dash of nutmeg

Heat the cider in a saucepan over a medium flame. While it's warming, rinse an Old-Fashioned glass with hot water and rim it with cinnamon. Pour the rum into the glass, and pop in the cinnamon stick. Then pour in the cider, and jazz it up with a thin orange slice slipped over the edge of the glass. Sprinkle cloves and nutmeg on top. Now, this is the way to get ready for winter!

COFFEE À LA MONTEGO BAY

*W*as it really invented in Jamaica? Who knows? But Coffee à la Montego Bay is just as warm and relaxing—it's a minivacation in a mug! And since it combines both rum and Tia Maria, this after-dinner favorite's sweetly strong. Try it with something dark and delicious, like a fudgy chocolate cake, chocolate gelato, or even tiramisu. Decadence!

1½ ounces dark rum
1 ounce Tia Maria
5–6 ounces black coffee
Dollop whipped cream
Few chocolate-covered espresso beans, for garnish

Warm a glass coffee mug by rinsing it with hot water and toss the rum and the Tia Maria into it. Grab the pot of fresh, preferably strong, black coffee, and add about 6 ounces, or less to taste (the less coffee the stronger the drink, of course). Mix with a spoon and top with plenty of whipped cream, and a few chocolate-covered espresso beans for an extra bang.

HEARTS AFIRE

*L*adies, this drink takes practice to perfect, but it's so worth it! Brandy's high alcohol content makes it flammable—done right, Hearts Afire is a stunning party drink, especially for a holiday celebration. But since you're playing with fire—literally—try it by yourself first so you're an expert by the time your shindig rolls around. You don't want to singe your guests with this fabulous, flaming concoction!

8 ounces brandy

12 ounces dark rum

3–4 tablespoons sugar

4 cups black coffee

Peel of ½–1 lemon, sliced very thin

3 cinnamon sticks

1–2 tablespoons whipped cream, optional

Warm the brandy and rum in a saucepan over a low flame. When it's warm, pour it into a large bowl with the sugar and lemon peel. Ignite the whole mix—making sure not to dip the match into the liquid! Stir the fiery mixture with a long, metal spoon while adding about 4 cups of good strong black coffee. When the flame's been extinguished, ladle into cups. Pop a cinnamon stick into each cup, then top with whipped cream.

THESE FIERY CONCOCTIONS ARE FUN TO MAKE AND THEIR EFFECT IS STUNNING when it's done well. But a couple of false moves, and more than just your heart will be set aflame! If you're an amateur, make sure to use a long match, the kind you'd light a fireplace with. To extinguish the flames, just stir with a metal spoon.

Café Royale

*Y*ou'll feel like royalty indeed when you end your dinner à *deux* with the most tantalizing of coffee concoctions. Set his heart—and his cup—on fire with tiny demitasse cups filled with java and bourbon. Even if you're not in love with, say, bourbon on the rocks or with cola, this dramatic drink will convert you for sure. Skip dessert, and whip up a pair of Café Royales instead.

2 sugar cubes (or 2 teaspoons sugar)   2 ounces 100-proof bourbon
8 ounces black coffee

Pop a sugar cube—or sprinkle 1 teaspoon of sugar—in the bottom of each espresso or demitasse cup. Then fill each nearly to the brim with coffee, carefully add the bourbon, and light her up using a long match. (Carefully, of course! Only pros should use lighters or household matches.) Stir each cup to extinguish the flames. Makes 2 sexy servings.

BOURBON—IT'S MEGAN'S BOOZE OF CHOICE. INTRODUCED TO IT ON HER 21st birthday by a well-meaning friend from Louisiana (who also taught her to smoke menthol cigarettes, and partake in a variety of other "healthy things"), she's been drinking it ever since. The stuff has its roots in Kentucky, where distillers have been making Bourbon whiskey (named after a "royal family" of France) since the late 18th century. Bourbon's smooth sweetness—which sets it apart from straight whiskey—comes from corn and barley.

MEGAN'S MOCHA

*Y*ou've had them plenty of times at all those coffee chains around your city, but have you ever made your own? There's no comparison! Don't wait in line—head home and whip up a few for brunch, or just for kicks on a quiet Sunday afternoon. Our recipe skips the booze, but you can add dark rum, coffee liqueur, or even vodka if you're not feeling, um, virginal . . .

¾ cup hot chocolate
⅛ teaspoon ground cinnamon
¾ cup black coffee

Dash of light cream, optional
Dollop of whipped cream, to top
Drizzle of chocolate syrup, optional
Drizzle of caramel sauce, optional

Warm an oversized mug with hot water (you know the routine!). Pour the hot chocolate, then the cinnamon, and finally the coffee into it. Add the light cream. (How much? Depends on how much time you want to spend at the gym later!) Mix well with a spoon, and top with a dollop of whipped cream. Try drizzling the whipped cream with chocolate syrup or caramel sauce, too.

YOU LOVE FRESH COFFEE, BUT YOU'VE GOT ZERO COUNTER SPACE IN THAT TINY kitchen of yours. Invest in a French press—available in most houseware stores for less than $30. It's a glass pot with a plunger, allowing you to brew coffee just as you would loose tea. The plunger presses the coffee grounds into the bottom of the pot, keeping your java full-bodied, rich, and free of gritty grounds. And it's the perfect size for storing in a cabinet—even in that shoebox-sized studio!

Café Brulot

Citrusy, sweet, and strong, this old-fashioned favorite features lemon and orange peels and cognac.

⅛ teaspoon lemon zest
⅛ teaspoon orange zest
1 teaspoon sugar
1 ounce cognac
4 ounces black coffee
Dollop whipped cream
1 orange peel, for garnish
A few whole cloves, for garnish

In a warm mug, muddle the lemon zest, orange zest, and sugar with a few drops of warm water. Add the cognac and mix well. Pour in the coffee. Although this is usually served jet-black with no cream, go ahead and top it with whipped cream if you've got a sweet tooth. Slip an orange twist over the rim of the mug or toss in a few whole cloves for an extra-festive touch.

EXERCISE IS ONE OF THE BEST THINGS YOU CAN DO FOR YOUR HUNGOVER self. Even if it sounds like the most painful thing in the world, get out of bed and get moving! Even a brisk walk helps, but it's best to break a sweat. Plus, it encourages you to drink more water, which'll rehydrate the hangover right out of you.

ALHAMBRA ROYALE

*A*round the holidays, our favorite gifts are those foil-wrapped chocolate "oranges" that are actually citrus-tinged balls of dark chocolate. It's such fun to share slices with someone special under the mistletoe. Alhambra Royales are the liquid version! Whip up a pair for you two to share; then snuggle up under the covers for a long winter's night.

1 cup hot chocolate	Dollop whipped cream
1 orange peel	Sprinkle of cinnamon
1½ ounces cognac	1 orange peel, for garnish

Fill a warm mug nearly full with hot chocolate, leaving space at the top, and add the orange peel. Warm the cognac, and ignite it in a ladle if you like, or do it the easy way, and simply add it to the hot chocolate (although you'll lose something in the presentation, it'll still taste just as great). Stir well, and top with as much whipped cream as you like. Sprinkle with cinnamon, and twist another orange peel around the edge. Delish!

Skip the storebought stuff—splurge on a batch of homemade whipped cream to add a luxurious touch to delicious hot drinks. First, chill a bowl and beaters from an electric mixer in the fridge for about 15 minutes. Then, combine ½ pint heavy cream, ⅓ cup powdered sugar, and ½ teaspoon vanilla in the chilled bowl. Beat until stiff, and *voilà!* You've got 2 cups of fresh, fluffy whipped cream that puts other versions to shame.

Mexican Coffee

We know, we know. You're thinking, tequila and coffee? No way! ¡Pero si! Erase those memories of too many tequila shots with this wonderfully tummy-warming coffee concoction. Makes a quick, easy dessert or afternoon indulgence if the weather's dark and stormy. And who can resist anything with oh-so-smooth Kahlua? Not us!

1½ ounces tequila
1 ounce Kahlua
4–5 ounces black coffee
Dollop whipped cream

Sprinkle of fresh coffee beans or chocolate-covered espresso beans, for garnish

Add the tequila and Kahlua to a warm glass coffee mug and stir gently. Pour in the black coffee, and top with plenty of sweet whipped cream. Want to jazz it up even more? Sprinkle fresh coffee beans or chocolate-covered espresso beans on top.

YOU WERE OUT ALL LAST NIGHT, GOT HOME AT THE BREAK OF DAWN; NOW IT'S noon, you're starving, and you just can't bear the thought of cooking, or even of leaving the house. And all you have in the fridge is cold pizza. Cold pizza! Combined with a cold diet soda—a type with plenty of caffeine—it's the hangover remedy of the gods. You'll feel like your chipper self in no time. (Hint: Stick with plain cheese pizza. Unless you have a stomach like a goat's, cold meats are dangerous first thing after waking up!)

Midnight Black

*M*olasses: We bet you've only used it in your ginger-bread recipe. Who knew it could be dark rum's new best friend? Here, its rich, deeply sweet taste is tempered by a touch of lemon and hints of cinnamon and nutmeg. Think of it as tea with extra benefits! Serve it with a spicy coffee cake, or even oatmeal raisin cookies. What a way to spend a winter afternoon.

4 ounces boiling water
2 teaspoons molasses
1 cinnamon stick
1 lemon peel
3 ounces dark rum
Sprinkle of ground nutmeg

Warm that glass coffee mug with boiling water, leaving a little in the bottom in which to dissolve the molasses. Add the cinnamon stick, the lemon peel, and the rest of the boiling water. Add the rum, and ignite for a few moments with a long match without dunking it in the drink. Stir, then top with ground nutmeg.

hen the mercury plummets, you're dying for drinks to warm both heart and tummy—of the guy sitting next to you on the couch, that is! You came to the right place. We bet you've already tried and loved our Hot Toddy, Gluhwein, Megan's Mocha, and most of the mug-worthy hot libations in this wintry chapter, so try making a few of your own. Coffee's just like hot vodka. Well, maybe not, but it is just as versatile as that particular spirit. And it goes with just about anything, so go ahead and experiment! You've never enjoyed the snow as much!

Chapter 6
For the Love of Chocolate

*I*t's so good. You can never get enough of it. And when you want it, you just have to have it.

We're talking about chocolate, of course, every girl's favorite vice. Next to booze, that is! That's why we couldn't resist mixing them in this melt-in-your-mouth chapter. Cocktails starting with chocolate make great pre- or post-dinner drinks, and can even double as liquid desserts. (After all, can you really handle the flourless chocolate torte *and* a Chocolate Martini? If the answer is yes, you're a stronger woman than either of us is!)

Dark and white crème de cacao take center stage here. Available at any liquor store, you'll want to buy a bottle of each to have on hand in case your honey wants to "come upstairs for a drink," or if your pals invade your pad demanding something decadent. (This happened to us once, and all we had on hand was a bottle of vodka. Oh, and some light beer. Our buddies left tipsy but disappointed.) Then see what other spirits you've got lying around . . . as you'll see in the next pages—and what you always knew—chocolate goes with just about anything.

ALTERNATINI

$\mathcal{N}$ot your run-of-the-mill, overly chocolaty concoction. (Not that we don't love those!) Vermouth and vodka balance the crème de cacao and chocolate garnish, and give this little indulgence a big kick. If you're not in the mood for a gooey dessert—or a drink that tastes like one—whip one of these up for yourself after dinner, or offer 'em to guests at your next dinner party.

Cocoa powder, to rim glass
3 ounces vodka
½ teaspoon sweet vermouth
½ teaspoon dry vermouth
1 teaspoon white crème de cacao
1 chocolate kiss candy, for garnish

Delicately dust rim of cocktail glass with cocoa powder. Pour liquid ingredients over ice in a perfectly chilled cocktail shaker. Shake, shake, shake, and strain into a cocktail glass. Don't forget to pop a chocolate kiss into the mix—unless you've already eaten the whole bag!

Angel's Kiss

This must be what one would taste like! It's time this old-fashioned recipe made a comeback. It's a great little dessert in itself, and it's also a yummy after-dinner drink. We like that it's small enough to sip two or three at the end of the night without falling asleep at the table. Try it as a special treat for birthdays or to celebrate that long-awaited promotion.

¼ ounce white crème de cacao
¼ ounce sloe gin
¼ ounce brandy
¼ ounce half-and-half

Layer each ingredient into a shot glass or small brandy snifter in the order listed. The effect will be tantalizing layers, as each liqueur floats on top of the other. The result? A heady, creamy miniature cocktail that looks as good as it tastes.

*"A woman drove me to drink,
and I hadn't even the courtesy to thank her."*
—W. C. Fields

Bourbon à la Crème

Who would've thought? (except us!) that chocolate is the perfect accompaniment to bourbon? But it's not chocolate milk or a run-of-the-mill milkshake. This devil of a drink is nothing less than iced indulgence. Even those of us who can't stand bourbon, say, on the rocks or mixed with cola will be thrilled and chilled. Give that Wild Turkey or Old Grandad a little class à la crème.

2 ounces bourbon
1 ounce dark crème de cacao
Sprinkle of vanilla beans, for garnish

Blend 'em all together with crushed ice, then chill in the refrigerator for 1 hour. Go get a manicure. By the time you get back, this deliciously sweet and slippery treat will be ready for you to try before heading out onto the town. Strain into a cocktail glass, top with vanilla beans, sit back, and sip.

Chocolate Malted

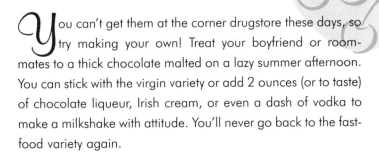

*Y*ou can't get them at the corner drugstore these days, so try making your own! Treat your boyfriend or room-mates to a thick chocolate malted on a lazy summer afternoon. You can stick with the virgin variety or add 2 ounces (or to taste) of chocolate liqueur, Irish cream, or even a dash of vodka to make a milkshake with attitude. You'll never go back to the fast-food variety again.

1 cup whole milk
2 scoops chocolate ice cream
¼ cup chocolate syrup
2 generous tablespoons malt powder
1 maraschino cherry, for garnish

Mix all ingredients in a blender until silky smooth. Pour into a chilled 10-inch glass (a pint glass will do nicely, too) and add straws. If yours is a virgin, garnish with a cherry. (Oops! did we say that?)

Is chocolate really an aphrodisiac? Well, although it contains no sexy substances that chemically increase your libido, it does contain mood-boosting tryptophan. Chocolate also releases your body's endorphins, which can give you a happy, glowing feeling similar to runner's high. (Or the high you get after a romp between the sheets!) We think these are great reasons to eat—and drink—up!

For the Love of Chocolate

MILK CHOCOLATE COCKTAIL

Okay, so we use cream, not milk. Who cares? Skip the skim milk and throw calories to the wind for once, and try this fabulously simple, yet indulgent, cocktail. Although it's great on its own, you can rim the glass with unsweetened cocoa, or float a few cocoa or coffee beans on top. Serve them up with light, desserty nibbles such as nuts, fresh raspberries, or other fresh fruit.

> 1 ounce gin
> 1 ounce crème de cacao
> 1 ounce heavy cream

Swirl gin, crème de cacao, and cream over cracked ice in a blender or shaker. Resist the urge to drink immediately! Shake it up and strain into a chilled cocktail glass.

So you've downed a few too many cocktails—chocolaty or otherwise—and this morning you don't exactly feel like you've gotten your beauty sleep. Our favorite cure is a chocolate chip muffin and a black coffee or a cola. The comfort food–caffeine combo lets you treat yourself while giving you the "pick-me-up" of your life. And what a great excuse to have even more chocolate!

THE CHOCOLATE-DIPPED ALMOND

We love the sweet and nutty flavor of amaretto, and it's a perfect match for decadent crème de cacao. Gin's clear, sharp taste makes this an impeccably balanced libation. Since it's gin-based, this Almond Joy-in-a-glass works wonderfully on its own or post-dinner.

1½ ounces gin   ½ ounce amaretto
½ ounce crème de cacao

Chill it! Put the whole mix into a shaker or blender over plenty of crushed ice, mix, and watch it glide into a cocktail glass. Make it for your date, but if you do, skip the blender—mixing it in a shiny metal shaker is so much sexier.

CRÈME DE CITY

Don't be fooled. Crème de City looks suspiciously like a martini, but it's way different. In a new take on an old-fashioned recipe, the gin and crème de cacao balance each other beautifully—just like you and your guy. True love in a glass. Sigh!

2 ounces gin   ¼ ounce crème de cacao
½ ounce dry vermouth

Over the rocks they all go; shake well. (A bartender once advised us to, "Really put yourself into it!") Pour into a martini glass, and just enjoy.

DEVIL IN A WHITE DRESS

No, we're not talking about you! We're talking about a kicked-up version of the Milk Chocolate Cocktail. This recipe adds white crème de menthe, which adds a hint of mint without altering the perfectly pale shade. It's mint chocolate chip ice cream, all grown up. Forgo the after-dinner mints—your lips will be more than kissable after one or two of these Devils.

1½ ounces gin
1 ounce white crème de cacao
½ ounce white crème de menthe
1 ounce heavy cream
1 mint sprig or pastel mints

Mix all ingredients—except the mint sprig and pastel mints—in a cocktail shaker over cracked ice. Gently strain into a cocktail glass, then float a few pastel mints on top, or pop a fresh mint sprig over the edge of the glass. Devilishly minty! Doesn't it feel good to be bad?

THE DEVIL MADE YOU DO IT! YOU BOUGHT THAT RED VALENTINO MINISKIRT— you might as well whip up something sinful to go along with it. It's a perfect match with the Devil in a White Dress. Price tags and calories be damned! Treat yourself.

White Russian

ou probably had one the first time you got drunk, made by a tipsy teenager at a house party. Try it again in "city-fied" style. After all, it's a classic (and it's so much nicer when it's not chasing several cheap wine coolers). One caveat: Don't order or make them at the end of the night, especially if you've been drinking beer or wine beforehand. In the wrong combination, the vodka and crème de cacao can make this Russian positively evil.

1½ ounces vodka
1 ounce white crème de cacao
¾ ounce heavy cream

Pour all ingredients over the rocks in a cocktail shaker. Shake it up (you're getting good at this by now!) and strain into a well-chilled cocktail glass. You'll be sending your love to Russia in no time flat.

MINT CONDITION

That's just how you'll feel after one or two of these concoctions. If it's something crisp you crave—like a liquid peppermint patty—eschew the traditional Grasshopper for something much more potent, and tempt your man with one of these take-no-prisoners treats. Sip while feeding each other morsels of dark chocolate—he'll thank you in the morning!

1½ ounces vodka
½ ounce chocolate liqueur (again, we love Godiva)
½ ounce crème de menthe

Skip the after-dinner mints! Just combine all ingredients in a cocktail shaker over ice, shake, and strain into a martini glass for a potent treat that's better than Junior Mints any day.

THE BEST KINDS OF CHOCOLATE TO PAIR WITH CHOCOLATE DRINKS? SOME OF the best are Teuscher (*www.teuscher.com*), which is Swiss; Neuhaus Chocolatier (*www.neuhauschocolate.com*), which is Belgian; and Ghirardelli (*www.Ghirardelli.com*), rich, delicious, and a bit less expensive, which is available in any grocery store in a pinch.

MINT CHOCOLATE CRUNCH

You can't get this "smoothie-with-attitude" at Baskin Robbins! So make it at home, on a sticky afternoon or a sultry evening. It's great for sipping anytime of the year, but if you're craving something cold and creamy during the summer months, this is our number-one recommendation. Now *this* is dessert done right.

1 ounce white crème de menthe
1–1½ ounces dark crème de cacao
1 cup vanilla ice cream or premium frozen yogurt
3 chocolate sandwich cookies, or to taste

Pop everything into a blender, and blend until cookies are crushed. (Don't blend too finely, or the cookie pieces will be too small, giving the drink a weird, grainy consistency.) Pour into a tall glass, stick a straw in, and crumble more cookie pieces on top. For a really head-spinning version, try adding 1–2 ounces vodka or vanilla vodka (carefully). Good to the last drop!

BANANA SPLIT

*W*hen your friends are sick of the same old Kamikaze shots or Lemon Drops, try your hand at one of these. These wicked little demons are sweet and deceptively smooth (which sounds like some of the men we know). We recommend having just one or two, though, or you'll pay the price in the morning. (Although it just might be worth it!)

1 ounce crème de banana	1 tablespoon whipped cream
1 ounce dark crème de cacao	Sprinkle of cocoa powder

Layer each ingredient in a shot glass, squirt lots of whipped cream on top, and dust with cocoa powder. Now knock it back! Using your hands is optional—sometimes using your mouth can be so much more fun!

YOU'RE IN VEGAS, BUT DON'T SPEND ALL YOUR CASH ON THE SLOT machines—make sure you've got some to spare on its fabulous nightlife! There's the **Velvet Lounge**—3355 Las Vegas Boulevard South, (702) 414-1699—a subtle, yet swank lounge, where you'll find myriad martinis from which to choose and a gorgeous patio to boot. The "V" in **V Bar**—3355 Las Vegas Blvd South, (702) 414-3200—must stand for "Very hip," with its dark sultry interior lit only by candles and colorful cocktails. And **Peppermill's Fireside Lounge**—2985 Las Vegas Boulevard South, (702) 735-7635—is *the* place to take a date, with huge comfy couches, 1970s-style, charm, and great Mai Tais! (For our equally great recipe, see page 48!)

La Linda

$\mathcal{E}$verything will look *linda* after sipping a couple of these creamy concoctions. Tequila and chocolate? Sounds, um, different. But trust us, it works. Tequila's surprisingly versatile, aside from margaritas or your average salt-and-lemon shot! This drink is especially effective after a long day at the office—booze and chocolate will give you just the attitude adjustment you need.

1–1½ ounces tequila
1 ounce white crème de cacao
3 ounces light cream or milk
Dash of grenadine

Pour all ingredients in a blender, add ice, and blend until silky smooth. Pour into a cocktail glass, add a straw, and indulge!

YOU'VE HAD A FEW CHOCOLATY COCKTAILS AND NOW YOU'RE IN THE MOOD for some sweet lovin'. Why not try chocolate body paint (available at many chocolate specialty and novelty stores)? But forgo the cute little brush, and keep the stuff in the kitchen—bet you didn't know it can double as delicious hot fudge! It doesn't come cheap, but it's definitely top quality. Spoon it over ice cream, cookies, brownies, or anything that tastes better with chocolate—that is, everything!

THE CHOCOHOLIC

*W*e know you're hard-core enough to handle one of these! Probably one of the richest drinks we've ever tasted, this cocktail makes Ben & Jerry's seem like child's play. Rich, nutty amaretto and seductively dark rum mix with crème de cacao to create the ultimate death-by-chocolate drink. Test your date: If he can handle one of these, you can be sure he's not faint of heart.

1–1½ ounces dark rum
1 ounce amaretto
½ ounce dark crème de cacao
1½–2 ounces cream
Cocoa powder, to rim glass
1 cocoa bean, for garnish

Pour all ingredients over ice (except the cocoa powder and cocoa bean, of course!) into cocktail shaker; shake well so it's nice and cold. Strain into a cocktail or martini glass. Try rimming the glass with cocoa powder, and garnishing it with a cocoa bean—the cocoa powder makes it that much more lickable!

"I can resist anything but temptation."
—Oscar Wilde (And chocolate, we'd like to add!)

Chocolate Cherry Kiss

$\mathcal{I}$f it's a shot or shooter you're after, skip the Jaeger and give this little gem a try. The complex flavors of the liqueurs still let the cherry-tinged grenadine explode in your mouth. Just don't forget to swallow! (Sorry, we couldn't resist.) But honestly, it's the best thing since chocolate-covered cherries or that famous ice-cream concoction named after Jerry Garcia.

¼ ounce dark crème de cacao
¼ ounce Irish cream
¼ ounce amaretto
¼ ounce Frangelico
Dash of grenadine
Dollop of whipped cream

Layer all ingredients in the order listed in a shot glass to make a mini-drink that's as pretty as it is delicious. You could give it a squirt or two of whipped cream for effect, but it's got the perfect amount of sweetness all by itself.

"Chocolate is a perfect food, as wholesome as it is delicious, a beneficent restorer of exhausted power. It is the best friend of those engaged in literary pursuits."
—Baron Justus von Liebig (1803–1873), German chemist

We know there are some people in the world who don't like chocolate, but we haven't met any yet! Hence, this decadent chapter on everyone's favorite indulgence. If you haven't tried the Chocolate Martini yet, put this book down, run out and buy the ingredients, and find out what you've been missing! (See our recipe on page 13.) Or if you're feeling like booze is old news try an old-fashioned Chocolate Malted, and you won't mind that there aren't soda fountains in every drugstore nowadays. And don't forget to pair chocolate with chocolate: Splurge on something rich and gooey to accompany your drink, and worry about hours spent on the treadmill tomorrow.

CHAPTER 7
COSMOPOLITANS, OF COURSE!

hat's in a name? Everything! The cosmopolitan, which has become the queen of cocktails over the past few years, isn't just your average girly drink. It connotes worldliness, inimitable style, sexy self-confidence—and, of course, the magazine that sports the same name.

Some say that the cosmo is "so five-minutes-ago.com." Are you one of them? In this chapter, we'll convince you to think again! The cosmopolitan's greatness lies in its versatility. There are tons of fun ways to dress it up, down, or any which way. You'll love the breeziness of a Cocopolitan, the fruitiness of a Watermelon Cosmo, and the pale-green sweetness of a Million-Dollar Melon Ball.

If you're like us, you always end up playing the role of hostess whenever you and your buddies are in the mood to party. (Probably because of your reputation as Party Goddess!) And those old standbys like light beer and white wine are just too darn ordinary sometimes. That's where these 21st-century cosmos come in. Try our recipes, then experiment and create your own.

The Classic Cosmopolitan

You loved it even before it was the drink of choice of a certain TV sexpot/writer named Carrie! Who'd have thought it'd be so easy to make? Here's a hint: since vodka's in the limelight here, stick with the quality stuff, and skip the plastic bottle bargain-basement variety. (Plus, we think the latter causes particularly horrid hangovers, so you'll thank us in the morning!)

2 ounces vodka
1 ounce triple sec
1 ounce cranberry juice
½ ounce fresh lime juice

Fill your trusty cocktail shaker with ice, and swirl the vodka, triple sec, cranberry juice, and lime juice into it. Shake well (don't forget to put the lid on first!) and gently strain into a cold martini glass. Guaranteed to steal the spotlight at your next fete.

YOU KNEW THAT TRIPLE SEC ADDS THAT GREAT CITRUSY FLAVOR TO DRINKS LIKE margaritas and such, but what exactly is it? Well, it's derived from distilling orange peels steeped in alcohol—"triple sec" means "distilled three times." Triple sec is a relative of the eye-stopping blue curaçao, and of Grand Marnier (which is slightly more expensive than the other two, since it's only produced in a small town in France). The difference? The type of oranges used to make each flavorful liqueur.

COINTREAU COSMO

This twist on the traditional cosmo takes your favorite cocktail from classy to classiest! With Cointreau's citrusy flavor, there's no need to add extra lime juice, except just a few drops from the lime wheel that graces the rim of your glass, perhaps. You can twist it seductively into the mix while you're chatting with the cute party-crasher who just arrived at your place . . .

2 ounces vodka
1 ounce Cointreau
1½ ounces cranberry juice
1 lime wheel

You know what to do: Fill your cocktail shaker with plenty of ice, and toss the vodka, Cointreau, and cranberry juice into it. (Feel free to alter the amount of cranberry juice to taste!) Shake it up and strain into an oh-so-cold cocktail glass. Liquid sex in *your* city!

WE KNOW YOU'RE WONDERING: "WHAT'S THE BEST WAY TO ACCESSORIZE MY cosmopolitan?" Well, Lulu Guinness has as many adorable handbags are there are recipes for cosmos! When we stopped by her store in the Soho area of Manhattan, we snagged a catalog and fell instantly in love on the subway ride home. Play a tough girl with a purse that features a pug dog, or keep it simple with a sleek black bag. Lulu's got one to match your every mood.

Cosmic Cosmo

When they're on a shopping expedition, Megan's best friend, Karen, teases her for grabbing anything that's sparkly off the rack (or the shelf, or the counter), and that goes for drinks, too. After all, who can resist the sparkle in champagne? A Cosmic Cosmo will heat up any evening. And it can even cool you down after you've thrown in the towel—we mean, credit card—and headed home from your own shopping spree.

1 ounce lemon vodka
½ ounce Cointreau
3 ounces champagne
Dash of cognac/fruit juice blend (one brand we like is Remy Red)

Remember, shaking champagne (or anything with bubbles) is a cardinal sin! First, swirl only the vodka and Cointreau in your trusty cocktail shaker, then strain into a chilled cocktail glass. Add the champagne, then top off with just a dash of cognac/fruit juice blend (what a great excuse to buy a bottle). Then get ready for a starry night.

COCOPOLITAN

*M*alibu rum—it's not just for sea breezes anymore! This lip-licking, coconutty liqueur—doesn't it just taste like the beach?—is enjoying its very own revival, especially as the costar of this summery take on the cosmopolitan. Enjoy this drink by itself, or serve with slices of fresh melon and kiwi. It'll be the life of your roofdeck party, we promise!

2 ounces vodka
1 ounce Malibu rum
1 ounce cranberry juice
Dash of Cointreau
1 coconut curl or 1 sprinkle of shaved coconut, for garnish

In your cocktail shaker filled with ice, toss the vodka, Malibu, cranberry juice, and Cointreau (go easy on the Cointreau so it doesn't overwhelm the Malibu). Shake, shake, shake; strain into a cocktail glass. Sprinkle coconut shavings or a coconut curl on top. Enjoy those summer days!

USE OUR BARSIDE ASTROLOGER TO FIND THE LIQUOR THAT BEST SUITS YOUR SIGN! Aries, you're a born leader; try crystal-clear vodka. Taurus, you're sensual and stubborn; let brandy tantalize your senses. Gemini, you're bright, talkative, and lively; sip sparkling champagne.

Watermelon Cosmopolitan

Ever since you had seed-spitting contests as a kid, water-melon has always been your favorite summertime fruit. And now that you're all grown up, what better way to enjoy it than in a cosmopolitan? If you're craving a Watermelon Cosmo in the winter, forgo the fresh fruit for watermelon liqueur—you'll find it in your liquor store.

1 ounce watermelon liqueur or 1 square inch watermelon
2 ounces lemon vodka
1 ounce cranberry juice

If you opt for the watermelon liqueur, simply pour all ingredients into your ice-filled cocktail shaker, and strain into that chilled cocktail glass. Instant gratification! If you're using fresh watermelon, muddle it in the bottom of the chilled cocktail glass with a little of the vodka. Then toss the rest of the vodka and the cranberry juice over ice in your cocktail shaker, shake well, and strain it over the muddled melon. Stir, sit back, and sip.

BAR-SIDE ASTROLOGER, CONTINUED. CANCER, YOU'RE EMOTIONAL AND YOU love the comforts of home; try cognac as a great after-dinner indulgence. Leo, you're a drama queen and the life of the party; try something wild, like cinnamon vodka. Virgo, you're detailed and practical; invest in some great single-malt scotch.

Peaches and Cream Cosmo

Peaches and cream—once upon a time, it described a perfect complexion; today it describes a sweet, delicious variation on the cosmopolitan theme. Peach nectar isn't hard to find. You can grab a can at your local deli, or a bottle at the grocery store. Need serving suggestions? Have your man over for dinner, and mix up a few of these afterward. Later, he'll want to have you for dessert!

2 ounces vanilla vodka	Dash of Cointreau or triple sec
1 ounce peach schapps	1–2 fresh peach slices
1 ounce peach nectar	

Got your cocktail shaker filled with plenty of ice? Swirl the vodka, peach schnapps, peach nectar, and Cointreau or triple sec into it, and give it a few good shakes. Strain the mix into an ice-cold cocktail glass and slide a fresh peach slice or 2 over the rim, just for fun. It's sinfully sweet—but you deserve it!

BAR-SIDE ASTROLOGER, CONTINUED. LIBRA, YOU'RE BALANCED AND LOVE being part of a couple; coffee and sweet liqueurs like Irish cream are perfect partners. Scorpio, you're intense, passionate, and brooding; try darkly sweet Kahlua. Sagittarius, you're open-minded and enthusiastic; take a chance, and try sambuca.

COSMOPOLITANS, OF COURSE!

JAZZBERRY COSMO

These little devils have proved to be downright addictive! After having two or three, it may seem like a good idea to declare your love for the poor, helpless man sitting next to you, and repeatedly demand to move in with him. Instead, whip up a few Jazzberry Cosmos for your next big shindig. Sip slowly, though—or you may end up with a new boyfriend whose name eludes you the next morning.

2 ounces raspberry vodka
½ ounce Cointreau
½ ounce fresh lime juice

1 ounce pineapple juice
1 pineapple or lime slice

Pour the raspberry vodka, Cointreau, lime juice, and pineapple juice into your ice-filled cocktail shaker, and shake it up. Grab a chilled cocktail glass and strain the mixture into it (although you'll probably want to drink it straight from the shaker!). Pop a slice of pineapple or lime over the edge, just to jazz it up a bit.

BAR-SIDE ASTROLOGER, CONTINUED. CAPRICORN, YOU'RE ORGANIZED, EFFIcient, and industrious; sip crisp, versatile gin. Aquarius, you're a freedom-loving visionary; spread your wings with summery Malibu rum. Pisces, you're spiritual and easygoing; relax with a quality tequila.

THAT LITTLE TART

It's what your father called your wild best friend in high school; now it's a cool cosmo-style cocktail, too! This cocky twist on the cosmopolitan shakes things up by substituting white cranberry juice for the red stuff, and adds a touch of sour mix for tartness. Syrupy-sweet, it's certainly not! Serve it as the house special when you throw that joint party with the guys across the hall.

2 ounces lemon vodka
1 ounce dash of white cranberry juice
½ ounce sour mix
½ ounce triple sec
A few fresh cranberries, for garnish

This concoction's pristinely pale shade shouldn't fool you—it's wicked! Mix the vodka, cranberry juice, sour mix, and triple sec in your cocktail shaker, and shake well. Gently strain into an ice-cold cocktail glass, and float a few fresh cranberries on top. Pucker up!

MEXICOSMOPOLITAN

We know; some of us absolutely cringe at the mention of the word "tequila." Don't worry, we're not talking about the famous tequila shot—we've dedicate page 151 to that! In this quirky cocktail, the vodka balances the tequila quite well, and orange juice helps everything go down smoothly. This drink makes a great alternative to the standard margarita. *Salud!*

1 ounce tequila
2 ounces lemon vodka
Drop of Cointreau or triple sec
1 ounce orange juice

This one is as easy as can be: just toss everything into a cocktail shaker over ice, shake to blend the vodka and tequila well, and then strain into a chilled cocktail glass.

FOR ALL-NATURAL HANGOVER RELIEF, TRY DRINKING PLENTY OF FRESH JUICES TO rehydrate your body and to rid it of toxins. If that doesn't do the trick, you might want to pick up nux vomica, an herbal supplement, from the nearest health food store. Take one every four hours to settle your stomach—you'll be good as new in no time.

MILLION-DOLLAR MELON BALL

Not only does the Million-Dollar Melon Ball taste like a million bucks, but it's also the color of cash! Bet you've only had Midori when it's been matched with sour mix. Well, it's time to expand your "spirit"ual horizons! This funky combination is a Midori sour and a cosmopolitan rolled into one melon-licious miracle of mixology.

2 ounces vodka
1 ounce Midori
½ ounce Cointreau
½ ounce sour mix
1 orange slice

In a cocktail shaker filled with ice, mix the vodka, Midori, Cointreau, and sour mix. After giving it a few good, hard shakes, strain it into a cold cocktail glass, and slip an orange slice over the edge. (The orange is such a cool contrast with bright green Midori!)

"Never drink in a revolving bar."
—Herman Rosen

Rum Rocker

Okay, so rum's MIA from your basic cosmo, but who says it has to be vodka-based or bust? Not us! This colorful cooler stars rum, with traditional cosmo elements Cointreau and cranberry as supporting actors. The result? A fresh, fruity cocktail with tons of flair. Remember, you heard it here first!

2 ounces lemon rum
1 ounce Cointreau
1 ounce cranberry juice
1 lemon slice

What could be easier? Just toss the rum, Cointreau, and cranberry juice in your cocktail shaker over ice and shake well. Gently swirl it into a chilled cocktail glass, pop a lemon slice over the rim, kick off your shoes, and relax.

IN NEW ORLEANS, A ROOM WITH A VIEW DOESN'T COME CHEAP, BUT IT'S worth it. **Club 360**—2 Canal Street, (504) 522-9795—is a great date spot, is the world's largest revolving bar/lounge, and it's got fab cocktails to boot. Or try **Lafitte's Blacksmith Shop**—941 Bourbon Street, (504) 523-0066—which is actually a cozy, candlelit spot that's frequented by locals, visitors, and celebrities. And at the upscale **Bombay Club**—830 Conti Street, (504) 586-0972—it's all about the tables for two and the fantastic quality martinis.

TOKYO COSMO

Sake, or Japanese rice wine, is showing up in all sorts of drinks, from sangria to martinis to—you guessed it!—cosmopolitans. Because its taste is so similar to vodka's, you can partner it with just about anything. In this drink, sake is part of a happy family when mixed with Cointreau, cranberry juice, and lime juice. Try this with all sorts of sushi, such as spicy tuna, inside-out California rolls, or eel with avocado.

2 ounces sake
1 ounce Cointreau
1½ ounces cranberry juice

Dash of fresh lime juice
1 lime slice

Grab your cocktail shaker, fill it with ice, and then add the sake, Cointreau, cranberry juice, and lime juice. Shake it up, then slowly pour into that chilled cocktail glass you've got waiting. Complete by twisting a juicy lime slice over the edge of the glass—your guests will surely say, *"Arigato!"*

SINCE 300 B.C., SAKE HAS BEEN THE DRINK OF CHOICE IN JAPAN, AND NOW it's made its way across the ocean to the United States. Also known as rice wine, sake is made the same way as American wine, but from fermented rice instead of fermented grapes. Associated with religious ceremonies, it still has a special place in Japanese society. It's served in beautiful cups reserved especially for sake. Serve slightly chilled. It's a great substitution for vodka in your favorite cocktail.

AMARETTOPOLITAN

Until Megan tried the Amarettopolitan, she really wasn't a fan of amaretto (the nutty almond liqueur from which this dreamy drink takes its name). "Plus," she thought, "amaretto with cranberry juice? Not a chance!" But the combination turned out to be sweetly, surprisingly refreshing, especially with a little vodka to liven things up. Go ahead and give it a shot!

> 2 ounces vodka
> 1 ounce amaretto
> 1 ounce cranberry juice
> Dash of fresh lemon juice
> Sprinkle of sliced almonds or 1 lemon slice, for garnish

Get ready to go nuts—literally! Pour the vodka, amaretto, cranberry juice, and lemon juice over plenty of cracked ice in your classy cocktail shaker, then strain into a nice, cold cocktail glass. Float a few almond slices on top, or keep it simple and slip a lemon slice over the rim of the glass. (If you're feeling extra creative, try rimming the glass with finely ground almonds, just as you would with sugar or salt!)

A Kissing Fool

No, we're not talking about the way your boyfriend acts when he's around you. (Or, are we?) We're talking about a brand-new, citrusy-sweet recipe for this quirky cosmo. You can't go wrong with romantic Chambord's raspberry sweetness, especially when you pair it with tart lemon juice, Cointreau, and vodka's crispness. Plan to whip some up for your next rendevous *à deux!*

2½ ounces vodka
1 ounce Chambord
½ ounce Cointreau

Dash of fresh lemon juice
2–3 fresh raspberries, for garnish

Fill that cocktail shaker with ice, then add the vodka, Chambord, Cointreau, and lemon juice. Shake it well—there're many flavors at play here, and all of them should harmonize! Strain into a cold cocktail glass. Pop a couple fresh raspberries on top, or perch them on the rim of the glass for garnish.

IF YOU WERE OUT LATE LAST NIGHT, TREAT YOURSELF TO A HOMEMADE BRUNCH (or have one delivered!) and mix up a classic Bloody Mary to go with it! Just combine the following over ice in a Collins glass: 2 ounces of vodka, 5 ounces of tomato juice, ¼ teaspoon Worcestershire sauce, a few dashes of Tabasco sauce, a pinch of pepper, and ¼ teaspoon chopped dill. Stir with a celery stick. No need to feel guilty—tomato juice is good for you!

Cosmopolitan Mandarin Martini

Sophisticated, chic, and very sexy, this pretty pink-tinged Cosmotini was created by longtime bartender Nancy Manchester for Glenn Chu's Honolulu restaurant, Indigo. This sleek drink is especially popular during *pau hana*, Honolulu's "happy hour," when locals and savvy visitors flock to the best watering holes to share delicious *pupus*, chat, and unwind. Thanks to Glenn and Nancy for this one!

1½ ounces orange vodka
½ ounce triple sec
¾ ounce sour mix
½ ounce Rose's lime juice
¾ ounce cranberry juice
1 lime slice, for garnish
1 orchid blossom, for garnish

It's important to get the proportions right for this drink! Fill a cocktail shaker with ice, and add everything but the lime slice and orchid blossom. Shake well, and strain into an ice-cold martini glass. Slide the lime slice over the rim of the glass and nestle the orchid blossom next to it. Tropically lovely!

ou thought Dr. Freud was right when he said, "A cosmo is just a Cosmo." Well, this chapter is proof that he's wrong! Who knew that there were tons of great variations on that standard city-girl cocktail? From the Cosmic Cosmo to the Peaches and Cream Cosmo, the possibilities are endless. And that makes them fun additions to any party! Why not have a cosmos-only party, and treat your guests to a few delicious, different kinds? Some may say the cosmopolitan has seen its day, but in our opinion, it's here to stay.

CHAPTER 8
DRINKS À DEUX

S o you're dating a new guy. You've gone out with him once or twice. He's funny, smart, knows how to dress, and actually listens to decent music. So far, so good. At least, you're pretty sure he's not Jack the Ripper.

But what's the ultimate 2-minute personality test for your date? Share a drink with him! That's right, girls. Forget those "Is Your Man Right for You?" quizzes—after just one drink with a guy, you'll know without a doubt if you want to ask him back to your place for another. If you're splitting a martini, does he hog all the olives? Snatch all the fresh strawberries from your Strawberry Margarita, and slug back the whole thing?

Then again, maybe he insists that you have the last sip of a mudslide, since you were saying you're a chocoholic. Maybe he brings over great champagne for the Champagne Cups you told him were on the menu, or a pint of class-A ice cream for Chocolate Passion Ice Creamies.

What's your man's S.Q. (Sharing Quotient)? Find out with these sensual, made-for-two recipes!

MUDSLIDE

You'll slide right into each other's arms as this decadently creamy treat slips down your throat. Don't even think about those premade, bottled types you see in liquor stores! This mudslide is the real deal, and it's got enough of a kick to prove it. Looking to nibble on something while you sip? Try chocolate-covered almonds, miniature truffles, or a bar of white chocolate.

3 ounces Kahlua
3 ounces Irish cream
3 ounces vodka
2 cups milk
Handful mini chocolate chips, for garnish

Fill your blender half full with ice. Pour in the Kahlua, Irish cream, vodka, and milk. (It's tempting, but try not to drink the ingredients first!) Blend until the mixture is semi-slushy, then pour it into large wine glasses. Sprinkle a handful of mini chocolate chips on top to jazz it up.

GRAND PASSION

Your knees are trembling and your heart is racing—could it be love? Maybe, or it could be this delectably fruity, deep-red cocktail. Invite him over to indulge in an evening of Grand Passion. Serve it before dinner, but be ready to skip the main course and head straight to the bedroom!

2 ounces light rum
2 ounces Malibu rum
2 ounces red passion (cognac–fruit juice blend)
1 ounce Cointreau
2–3 coconut curls, for garnish

Fill your sleek silver cocktail shaker with ice, and swirl the rum, Malibu rum, red passion, and Cointreau into it. Shake it up. Pour the luscious mix into a pair of chilled martini glasses. Pop coconut curls over the rims of the glasses, or just serve it straight up.

THE WAY TO A MAN'S HEART IS DEFINITELY THROUGH THIS RECIPE FOR FUDGE. (It's worked for Megan countless times!) In a large pot, combine 4½ cups of sugar and 1 large can of evaporated milk. Bring it to a boil, reduce the heat, and stir in 1 stick of butter, 1½ bags semisweet chocolate chips, 1 bag of marshmallows, and 1 teaspoon of vanilla. Mix until it's smooth, then pour into a greased pan and chill for at least 4 hours. Makes 5 whole pounds of chocolate decadence!

DRINKS À DEUX

LEILANI'S LIQUID LUNCH

Guaranteed to light your fire, this tropical libation will cool both of you down on a sweaty summer day. Go ahead, linger over a light lunch and serve this Liquid Lunch as a fruity dessert. But beware, the overproof rum really makes this drink devilishly strong! Skip it if you like; you won't lose out on taste.

3 ounces light rum
1 ounce 151-proof rum
1 ounce blackberry liqueur
1 ounce fresh lemon juice
2 ounces fresh lime juice
6 ounces chilled pineapple juice
2 maraschino cherries, for garnish
2 pineapple wedges, for garnish

Toss both kinds of rum, blackberry liqueur, lemon juice, and lime juice into your ice-filled cocktail shaker. Strain into 2 Collins glasses over ice, and add the pineapple juice to each. Pop a cherry on top, or perch a pineapple wedge on the edge of the glasses.

HOT AND DIRTY MARTINIS

*Y*ou know that's just how he likes them! This peppery, briny, biting martini is great over savory appetizers— order in from your favorite sushi restaurant, or serve salty snacks like pretzels or chips. Pepper vodka does quite a job on your breath, but don't let that stop you from getting close. (That's why you're drinking them together!)

3–4 jalapeño slices, for garnish
6 ounces pepper vodka
½ ounce olive brine
4–6 green olives or to taste, for garnish

Rub the rims of 2 chilled cocktail glasses with a jalapeño slice. Toss the pepper vodka and olive brine into your cocktail shaker filled with ice. Shake well (pepper vodka is terrible when it's not ice-cold!) and strain into the glasses. Pop a couple olives into each, and slide a jalapeño slice over the edge of the glass.

Deep Thought #121:
"I love to drink,
but I hate to be hung over."
—Pat Buckley

Scorpion Bowl

*Y*es, just like the wicked little creature for which it's named, this drink can sting! When we ordered a Scorpion Bowl at a bar in Boston, it was served in a huge bowl with plenty of ice and several straws—it was quite a challenge. Our recipe's not nearly as daunting, but rest assured it'll make the two of you very happy. What inhibitions?

    4 ounces light rum
    2 ounces brandy
    3 ounces fresh lemon juice
    3 ounces orange juice
    2–3 lemon and orange slices

Pour the rum, brandy, lemon juice, and orange juice over ice in your cocktail shaker. Shake well so it's nice and cold. Strain it into a pint glass half filled with ice. Slide the fruit slices on the rim, slip 2 straws into it, and sip it together.

A ROOM FOR TWO

He wanted to come upstairs for a drink . . . why don't you skip the basic cocktails or coffee, and give him more than he bargained for with this twist on the traditional piña colada? Sure, it's not a one-second wonder, but it's worth a bit of work. And it's so sweet and smooth you'll have him asking for more, and more, and more . . .

4 ounces vodka
2 ounces light rum
1 ounce white crème de cacao
4 ounces orange juice
2 ounces passion fruit juice

1 ounce pineapple juice
1 ounce coconut milk
1 maraschino cherry, for garnish
Sprinkle of coconut shavings, for garnish

Fill your blender two-thirds full of ice, then swirl in the vodka, light rum, crème de cacao, juices, and coconut milk. Blend until it's nice and slushy, and pour the magnificent mix into a pint glass. (Or, better yet, a coconut shell!) Top with a cherry, or sprinkle with shaved coconut.

"Wine comes in at the mouth,
And love comes in at the eye;
That's all we shall know for truth,
Before we grow old and die."
—William Butler Yeats

CHOCOLATE PASSION ICE CREAMIES

See Girl. See Boy. See Girl and Boy sip Chocolate Passion Ice Creamies. See sparks fly! Invented by a woman well versed in the laws of romance, these icy treats shouldn't be mistaken for plain old dessert. The creator—who shall remain nameless to prevent too much fan mail—swears that they're regular elixirs of love. See for yourself!

4 ice cubes
1½ ounces Irish cream
1½ ounces dark crème de cacao
1½ ounces Frangelico
1½ ounces Kahlua
½ cup chocolate ice cream
½ cup milk

Toss the ice cubes in your blender, then add the Irish cream, crème de cacao, Frangelico, and Kahlua. Top with the chocolate ice cream and milk, then blend until icy and smooth. Pour into a pint glass, add 2 straws, and sip together.

NEED A RECIPE FOR INSTANCE ROMANCE? CLASSICALLY ROMANTIC MOVIES! Have your favorites on hand to pop into the DVD player, then just curl up with a couple of cocktails. We love *Casablanca*, starring Humphrey Bogart and Ingrid Bergman in sultry Morocco; *Lady and the Tramp*, one of Disney's all-time best (are you serving spaghetti for dinner?); and the ultra-sensual *The Piano*, featuring Holly Hunter and Harvey Keitel.

BRANDY RIPPLE

Tease his taste buds with a Brandy Ripple! Smooth, creamy, and as chocolaty as an ice-cream sundae (but with a very wicked kick), this sized-for-sharing drink/dessert makes a great end to a romantic dinner or a treat on a lazy afternoon. Still hungry? Dunk chocolate chip cookies into your Ripple, then feed them to each other. Sweet!

1 cup premium vanilla ice cream
3 ounces brandy
3 ounces dark crème de cacao

½ cup milk
Cocoa powder, to rim glass

Scoop the ice cream into the blender, then add the brandy and crème de cacao. Toss in the milk; blend for just a few seconds until it's milkshake-smooth. Serve it in a pint glass. If you're both real chocolate addicts, rim the glass with cocoa powder. Don't forget a pair of straws!

ON MEGAN'S MOST RECENT TRIP TO ONE OF THE TWIN CITIES, SHE WENT bowling and drank too much beer. But she wishes she'd found the well-hidden **Bev's Wine Bar**—250 3rd Avenue North, (612) 337-0102—an elegant, yet intimate, wine bar with very reasonable prices. Then there's the ultra-mod **Bobino Starlite Lounge**—212 East Hennepin Avenue, (612) 623-3301—with plenty of funky couches and booths perfect for a drink à deux. And celebs hang at oh-so-sophisticated **The Lounge**—411 2nd Avenue North, (612) 333-8800—which boasts Class-A DJs and a hot dance floor.

DRINKS À DEUX

WHITE VELVET KISSES

One note of caution: After one sip of a White Velvet Kiss, you won't want to leave the house! Grab your man, lock the door, dim the lights, and kiss over a couple of Kisses. These creamy concoctions are especially good before dinner. Who'd have thought your average-joe gin could be so sexy?

4 ounces gin
1 ounce crème de banana
2 ounces pineapple juice

1 ounce light cream
Dash of grenadine
2–3 maraschino cherries, for garnish

Pop the gin, crème de banana, pineapple juice, and cream into your handy cocktail shaker. Shake it up, then gently strain into perfectly chilled cocktail glasses. Drizzle a few drops of lipstick-red grenadine on top, and toss a couple of cherries into each glass. Then get comfortable . . .

IF YOU'RE HAVING HIM OVER FOR AN INTIMATE DINNER AND A QUIET EVENING for two, you'll want to choose just the right music to help set the mood! You can't go wrong with a little great jazz, like the smooth sounds of Dinah Washington and Billie Holiday. Or spin some of Frank Sinatra's old-school charm—it's just the thing for a little after-dinner dancing. And slip some Sting into the CD player before cuddling on the couch to set a soft, mellow mood.

Southern Peach

*ven if it's the middle of winter, these peachy-keen drinks will transport both of you to a sunny porch swing on a summer afternoon. Schedule a day to play hooky with your new man, then treat yourselves to a couple of these, and get to know each other better. We promise it won't take long!

2 ounces bourbon
1 ounce Southern Comfort
½ ounce peach schnapps
½ ounce fresh lemon juice

½ teaspoon sugar
Dash of club soda
1 fresh peach slice, for garnish

Swirl the bourbon, Southern Comfort, peach schnapps, lemon juice, and sugar into your cocktail shaker over ice, and shake well. (Make sure the sugar's dissolved!) Pour it into a Collins glass half full with fresh ice, and top with club soda. Then slip a peach slice over the edge of the glass. Perfect! (Serves 1)

SOUTHERN COMFORT—YOU'VE USED IT IN TONS OF DRINKS LIKE LONG Island Iced Tea and the Southern Peach, but what is the stuff? It's actually a form of bourbon infused with other flavors, such as peach and orange. Although the recipe is top secret, we know that it was originally created by a Louisiana bartender in 1870. Today it's produced in Kentucky, the birthplace of other great bourbons. Whatever you do, don't mix SoCo with diet cola. It's a mistake we made once, and have lived to regret it!

CHAMPAGNE CUP

Nothing puts you in the mood like champagne—it can turn any ordinary dinner into a real event. Pick a Saturday night, make sure your roommates will be out of town, and invite him over for dinner. Open a bottle and mix up a couple of these before dinner; then save the rest for dessert, and serve it with great chocolate and a bowl of nuts.

1 ounce white curaçao
½ ounce cognac
4 ounces champagne
1 orange slice, for garnish

Got your cocktail shaker? Great! Pour the curaçao and cognac into it, then shake well to mix and chill. Pour it into a champagne flute, and fill it up with cold champagne. Add an orange slice, and you've got instant elegance. (Serves 1)

WHAT'S MORE ROMANTIC THAN LOVE POETRY? IF YOU'VE GOT A GREAT anthology of love poems, keep it on the coffee table, and tell him to flip through it while you're mixing up cocktails—it'll put him in the mood for sure. If you haven't got such a collection, get your hands on these classic-not-cliché poems: "I Want to Say Your Name" by Leopold Senghor; "My Luve's like a Red, Red Rose" by Robert Burns; and "Steps" by Frank O'Hara. Then slip a copy into his bag, or into a cute card. He'll melt!

STRAWBERRY MARGARITA *PARA LOS NOVIOS*

Whip up one of these sexy "margs" for your new novio—Spanish for sweetheart—and you'll have him swooning in mere minutes. Since this oversized recipe doesn't skimp on the tequila (we'd never dream of doing that), you'll have plenty to share. But we're sure you'll be seeking seconds in—well, seconds. For an extra extravagant touch, substitute Grand Marnier for the triple sec.

Sugar or salt, to rim glass
4 ounces tequila
1 ounce triple sec
1 ounce strawberry schnapps
2 ounces lime juice
1–2 fresh strawberries

Rim a large wine glass with sugar or salt; either one works well. Toss the tequila, triple sec, strawberry schnapps, and lime juice into your ice-filled cocktail shaker. Shake well, then pour the yummy mix into the glass. Slip a couple of strawberries over the rim of the glass, and you're good to go. For extra kick, hollow out a lime, float it on top of the drink, and fill it with tequila. Good thing you're sharing!

FOR THE PERFECT MARGARITA, STICK WITH GOOD-QUALITY TEQUILA, FOR GREAT taste and to minimize tomorrow's headache. We like Cuervo Gold 1800. Of course, if you let a waiter buy you shots of the stuff at the end of your bartending shift, you're just asking for it, even if it's quality booze. (Not that we'd ever do anything as foolhardy as *that*.) Moral of the story? Don't try to find the worm at the bottom of the bottle.

CHERRY ALIVE

weet and buzzingly refreshing, this rich cherry-laced milkshake-esque treat tastes even better with two straws. Try it on a sweaty summer afternoon, or whenever the craving strikes you. And don't forget to pair it with something chocolaty, like fudge brownies or even a couple of chocolate candy kisses.

2 scoops premium vanilla ice cream or chocolate cherry ice cream
3 ounces vanilla vodka
½ cup light cream
12 maraschino cherries
1 ounce maraschino cherry juice or maraschino liqueur

Scoop the ice cream into the blender, then add the vodka, cream, cherries, and cherry juice or liqueur. Blend for a few seconds, just until the ice cream and cream are combined and the cherries are pulverized. On the wagon? No problem. Just omit the vodka, and use the cherry juice in place of the liqueur. It's still sensational.

$\mathcal{Y}$es, ladies, your grandmother was right: The way to a man's heart is through his stomach. (For that matter, it's a way to a woman's heart, as well.) And after reading this chapter, you should have it made. Did you knock him over with a well-timed Leilani's Liquid Lunch? Or maybe you sweet-talked him with Chocolate Passion Ice Creamies. Either way, these made-for-two drinks are definitely aphrodisiacs. Now try this at home! Create an oversized concoction using your favorite flavors, and see if he comes running. (What's that noise? Could it be the sound of men beating down your door? Yes!)

CHAPTER 9

HOOCH FOR THE HOLIDAYS

O ne of the best parties Megan's ever thrown was her State of the Union Address party. Yes, you read right. In order to suffer through a couple hours of what's generally boring-as-cardboard presidential rambling, a few friends and a few drinks are very much in order. So a few e-invites and a trip to the liquor store later, bam! A party was born. Okay, so her drink of choice that day was good old-fashioned American beer—not quite as creative as the lip-licking choices in this chapter. Nonetheless, it just goes to show that there's no holiday too big or too small to celebrate. (Yes, every party-giving addict knows there's always an excuse for a celebration!)

Well, we're all in luck, ladies, just about every day's a holiday of sorts. Let the games begin! Here, you'll find a colorful cocktail to brighten your Easter; a sweet trick-or-treat martini for your Halloween party; a St. Patrick's Day special that'll send you all the way back to Eire; and many more. Happy holidays!

State of the Union Address: Painkiller

You know you should watch the State of the Union Address, especially since the president only presents it once a year, and since you live in the Union yourself. (But why does it always seem to knock your favorite prime-time show off the air?) Liven things up by throwing a party and mixing a Painkiller for everyone. Even if you voted for the other guy, this drink will make the whole event much more fun.

2 ounces gin
2 ounces vodka
½ ounce triple sec

Splash cranberry juice
Spritz club soda

Grab an Old-Fashioned glass and fill it halfway with ice. Add the gin, vodka, and triple sec; stir, and toss in the cranberry juice. A spritz of club soda, and you've got a yummy, bubbly drink that's guaranteed to get you through the longest of presidential speeches.

THERE'S NOTHING QUITE LIKE A HOLIDAY HANGOVER. YOU'RE PROBABLY STILL stuffed from last night's feast, so take it easy today! We recommend eating lightly—dry, whole-wheat toast with egg whites for breakfast, a salad for lunch, and vegetable soup for dinner. Snack on fresh strawberries between meals; they're touted as a terrific hangover cure by many. All those good-for-you fruits and veggies will revitalize both body and soul.

Valentine's Day: Cupid's Elixir

*L*ove is in the air! But instead of the usual sticky-sweet drinks, try sexy, spicy Cupid's Elixir. It features decadent Goldschlager, and you'll love the tiny flecks of real gold floating in this pale golden mixture. Pour one for your man at the end of the evening—its cinnamony kick is guaranteed to put you in the mood.

2 ounces cinnamon vodka
1 ounce vodka
1 ounce Goldschlager
Sprinkle of miniature cinnamon hearts

Get your hands on that cocktail shaker, and toss plenty of cracked ice into it. Swirl the cinnamon vodka and vodka over it, give it a few good shakes, and strain it into a cold cocktail glass. Slowly add the Goldschlager and pop in a couple of mini cinnamon hearts for good measure. Here's to you!

VALENTINE'S DAY—IT'S A HOLIDAY FOR LOVERS, AND THE SCOURGE OF SINGLE folk. But why St. Valentine, and why February 14? Well, the good St. Valentine was a priest in Rome who was martyred on February 14, the eve of the feast of Lupercalia, in 270 A.D. On this Roman holiday, boys picked dates for the feast by drawing names out of a jar, and these blind dates often resulted in marriage. Who knew *The Dating Game* had its roots in ancient Rome?

PRESIDENTS' DAY: CHERRY TREE MARTINI

We cannot tell a lie: Neither George Washington nor Abraham Lincoln invented this bright-red cocktail—we did! And we didn't even have to chop down a cherry tree à la G.W., to do it. Enjoy your day off, and lift your glass to America's presidents with this easy-to-make take on the classic martini.

3 ounces vodka
1 ounce maraschino liqueur
1 maraschino cherry, for garnish

Fill your cocktail shaker with ice, and add the vodka and maraschino liqueur. Shake well, then strain the cherry-red mix into a chilled cocktail glass. Feeling patriotic? Stick a tiny American flag toothpick into a maraschino cherry, and pop it over the edge of the glass.

St. Patrick's Day: The Irish Temper

Everyone knows the Irish are famous for being expert partiers; just ask anyone who comes from an Irish family. And for Irish-Americans, St. Patrick's Day is an opportunity to do some serious celebrating. What St. Patty's *flea* (Gaelic for "drinking party") would be complete without Guinness and Irish whiskey? Be forewarned, though—this wicked mix is not for the faint of heart.

1 ounce Irish whiskey (try Bushmills or Powers)
1 ounce Irish Mist liqueur
1 can Guinness stout

Toss the Irish whiskey and the Irish Mist into a cold pint glass. Slowly add half of the Guinness; stir gently. (No one likes flat beer!) Add the other half of the Guinness, and let settle. Sip slowly—it might not taste like it, but remember, this pint's got extra kick!

Celebrate the feast day of St. Patrick, the legendary saint who drove dangerous snakes out of Ireland! It's also the day to celebrate the great beers for which Ireland's famous. Guinness, featured in the Irish Temper, is the drink of choice for Irish tipplers from Dublin to Galway Bay. It was Megan's drink of choice, too, when she went out on the town one night in Kanturk, County Cork, with the mother of a friend, who was at least 40 years her senior. By the end of the evening, after many pints of Guinness, Mrs. Culley was bright and chipper, while Megan was dying to hit the hay. Keep this in mind on March 17th: Guinness is so smooth that it's easy to slug back one too many!

Mardi Gras: Louisiana Hurricane

*E*ven if you can't get to New Orleans for this infamous festival, celebrating Mardi Gras—or Fat Tuesday—in your city is just as much fun when you add Hurricanes to the mix. To add an authentic "'Nawlins" touch to your party, order a king's cake from a bakery—it's a delicious ring-shaped coffee cake that traditionally has pennies baked inside. If you find one in your slice, you can look forward to luck for the upcoming year.

1 ounce light rum
1 ounce gold rum
½ ounce passion fruit syrup
½ ounce lime juice

Grab your cocktail shaker, fill it with cracked ice, and toss in the light rum, gold rum, passion fruit syrup, and lime juice. Shake it up, and strain into a chilled cocktail glass. For an especially stormy Hurricane, double the recipe, add a dash of cranberry juice, and serve on the rocks. Get ready to celebrate!

APRIL FOOL'S DAY: THE JOKER IS WILD!

What's the most heinous April Fool's trick a friend (or enemy!) ever pulled on you? We've had our fair share, and in our opinion, April Fool's Day is absolutely ridiculous. Practical jokes are so childish. We're way too sophisticated and refined to play pranks on anyone. Who invented such a silly holiday, anyway?

2 ounces banana liqueur
1 ounce crème de menthe
2 ounces Scotch
Dash of Guinness stout
½ ounce grenadine

Fill your cocktail shaker with ice, and add the banana liqueur, crème de menthe, and scotch. Strain into an oversized martini glass, and top with cold Guinness stout. Drizzle with grenadine. Yum!

What? You don't like it?

April Fool's! Instead of this stomach-churning combo, which you could whip up for *your* worst enemy, indulge in something foolproof today, like a microbrew or a glass of great wine.

Easter: Fuzzy Bunny

*W*ho wouldn't like to find a Fuzzy Bunny in her Easter basket? The Easter Bunny himself would be proud of this pretty little concoction. Plus, who needs an excuse to eat jellybeans? Invite friends over for Easter dinner, and keep them happy while dinner's cooking with a few of these.

1 ounce vodka
½ ounce peach schnapps
4 ounces rose champagne
2–3 miniature jellybeans, for garnish

Swirl the vodka—preferably chilled—into a cold champagne flute, then add the peach schnapps. Fill 'er up with champagne, and drop a couple colorful jellybeans into the mix. It's springtime!

WHAT'S THE BEST WAY TO MAKE A BAD HANGOVER WORSE? SMOKE WHEN you're drinking. You'll wake up thirsty, headachy, tired, and you'll have a sore throat. Oh, that doesn't sound like fun to you? Then put down the ciggies! Smoking and drinking is an enticing but deadly combination, so nip that habit in the butt. We guarantee you'll feel better in the morning.

Cinco de Mayo: Champagne Sangria

Happy Mexican Independence Day! Cinco de Mayo celebrates the anniversary of the stunning victory of the vastly outnumbered Mexican soldiers against Napoleon's troops on May 5, 1862. And the date still calls for one heck of a celebration today, with delicious food (and lots of it!) and great drinks. Mix a pitcher of delicious Champagne Sangria, then head out to your favorite Mexican restaurant to continue the fiesta.

1 orange, sliced	1 bottle dry champagne, chilled
1 apple, sliced	1 ounce triple sec
2 ounces vodka	A few dashes of lime juice, or to taste

Toss the sliced orange and apple into a pitcher; add the vodka. Slowly pour the champagne over the whole mix. (Tilt the pitcher to keep the champagne's foam to a minimum.) Add the triple sec and lime juice to taste—if it's too tart, add more triple sec, and if it's too sweet, add more lime juice. Stir gently, and serve in large wine glasses. (Great for brunch, too!)

Sangria has its roots in Spain, as does graceful, sensual flamenco dancing. The traditional dance of Gypsies in southern Spain, flamenco dancing looks easy, but its many subgenres are each made up of complicated toe-and-heel-clicking routines. The tradition of flamenco dancing has a mysterious side to it, too—no one is certain how elements of European, African, Asian, and Indian dance all combined to form flamenco. It could be the most multicultural form of dance in the world. Flamenco classes are offered everywhere—give them a try!

4th of July: Stars and Stripes Forever

*W*hat's the best way to honor America's birthday? With a drink in hand, of course. Celebrate Independence Day with a drinkable flag. This fun cordial actually creates red, white, and blue stripes. It's a great addition to your annual barbecue—and a great excuse to pick up delicious liqueurs that are anything but run-of-the-mill.

½ ounce crème de cassis
½ ounce green chartreuse
½ ounce maraschino liqueur

In a shot glass, layer all the ingredients in the given order. (For best results, pour the liqueur down the side of the shot glass—if you can do it neatly.) Serve with a sparkler!

You won't escape Miami's heat at **The Red Room**—394 Giralda Avenue, Coral Gables, (305) 445-5858—a hotspot that's too hot to handle! Instead, you'll salsa the night away while sipping delicious drinks, Latin-style. But if you want to cool down over a martini, hit **Mbar**—500 Brickell Key Drive, (305) 913-8288—a simply decorated bar featuring more than 250 (count 'em!) martinis. Looking for a more relaxed atmosphere? Try **Purdy Bar**—1811 Purdy Avenue, (305) 531-4622—which has fantastic cosmos and margaritas at even better prices.

Bastille Day: Montalembert Cocktail (from Montalembert Hotel in Paris)

*V*ive le France! Every July 14th, the French celebrate the anniversary of the storming of the Bastille prison during the French Revolution more than 200 years ago. Mix up a few Montalembert Cocktails, the specialty of a fabulous Parisian hotel, and serve them with a platter of Camembert and Brie, fresh fruit, and bowls of steamed *moules* (mussels). *Magnifique!*

2 ounces rum
1 ounce amaretto
½ ounce Cointreau
½ ounce lemon juice
Squirt of tonic water

Fill that cocktail shaker with ice, then add the rum, amaretto, Cointreau, and lemon juice. Shake, shake, shake, and strain into an ice-cold cocktail glass. Add just a squirt of tonic water, and you'll agree it's *très, très bon!*

Labor Day: Frozen Scotch Sours

*A*h, Labor Day—the holiday that celebrates work by, well, not making you do any. Keep that spirit alive if you're having a roofdeck barbecue or a party! These icy, refreshing Scotch Sours take just minutes to make, and use only a couple of basic ingredients, so you can spend more time with your buddies—enjoying the last days of summer—and less time behind the bar.

6-ounce can frozen lemonade
1 can water (use the empty lemonade can to measure)
1 can Scotch (use the empty lemonade can to measure)
4–6 maraschino cherries, for garnish
2 teaspoons (or to taste) maraschino cherry juice, for garnish
4–6 orange slices, for garnish

Get your blender ready to rumble, then fill it three-quarters full of ice. Pop in the frozen lemonade, water, and scotch. Blend until the mixture's reached a slushy consistency. Slowly pour into Old-Fashioned glasses. Toss a cherry and a drizzle of cherry juice into each, and slip an orange slice over the side. Serves 4 to 6 on those last precious days of summer.

HALLOWEEN: CANDY BAR COCKTAIL

You're never too old to trick or treat! Celebrate your sweet tooth with a decadent cocktail instead of those fun-sized candy bars. Have a Halloween party featuring the Candy Bar Cocktail, but beware of ghoulishly thirsty party-crashers! Serve this drink alongside bowls of candy corn, chocolate candy kisses, and other splurge-worthy treats.

2 ounces vodka
1 ounce Frangelico
1 ounce chocolate liqueur

Dash of cream
Drizzle of caramel topping

In your ice-filled cocktail shaker, pour the vodka, Frangelico, and chocolate liqueur. Shake while doing the Monster Mash; strain into a chilled cocktail glass. Add a dash of cream on top for a smoky, mysterious touch, and drizzle a bit of caramel sauce over it. Happy Halloween!

HALLOWEEN ROLLS AROUND EVERY YEAR, AND EVERY YEAR YOU SHOW UP TO Halloween parties in jeans because you just can't be bothered to dream up the perfect costume! Well, we've done the work for you. Be a French maid—grab a cheap feather duster from the grocery store, add heels, fishnets, a short black skirt, and a tummy-baring black tank top. Or strut your stuff as a bunny—throw on a leotard, tights, stilettos, a pair of bunny ears, and make a tail out of cotton balls. Inspired? Now dream up creative costumes of your own!

THANKSGIVING: PILGRIM'S PROGRESS

We've all been there. Even though you love them, there's definitely such a thing as too much family, especially around the holidays. Don't let it get to you—lighten the mood by offering to mix up a few of these tart cran-appletinis (even for Mom and Dad). Everyone will be giving thanks to you!

2 ounces vodka
1 ounce sour apple liqueur
1 ounce cranberry juice
Ground cinnamon, to rim glass
1 green apple slice, for garnish

It's a good thing you threw your cocktail shaker in your suitcase for this holiday trip! Fill it with ice, then pour in the vodka, sour apple liqueur, and cranberry juice. Relieve holiday stress by shaking well, then strain into a cinnamon-rimmed cocktail glass. Slide an apple slice over the edge and relax.

"Eat your bread with gladness,
and drink your wine with a merry heart."
—Ecclesiastes

CHRISTMAS DAY: EGGNOG

Never seen Santa Claus? Skip the milk and cookies, and leave him a glass of this Eggnog, and he'll stay around to thank you on Christmas morning. And this holiday staple is practically foolproof. One note of Christmas caution: Raw eggs can be tricky, so you might want to omit the yolks altogether, and use pasteurized egg whites (available in your grocery store).

6 eggs
½ cup sugar
3 cups milk
½ cup heavy cream, whipped

½ bottle brandy
Ground nutmeg, for garnish
Ground cinnamon, for garnish

If you're using eggs, separate them and set the whites aside. Beat the egg yolks with the sugar in a punch bowl, then stir in the milk and whipped cream. (Or just mix the milk and whipped cream together.) Pour in the brandy and chill for 1 hour. Right before you serve it, whip the egg whites until they form stiff peaks, and mix them into the Eggnog. Sprinkle as much nutmeg and cinnamon as you wish on top. Serves 10.

MISTLETOE—IT'S ALWAYS BEEN A GREAT EXCUSE TO SNAG A KISS FROM THAT CUTIE at your Christmas party! But the curious plant was once banned by the Catholic Church in England because it was considered a sign of paganism. On one Christmas Day in the 17th century, though, a revolutionary English minister proclaimed it to be a sign of goodwill; later, Victorian lovers interpreted "goodwill" as "stealing a kiss"!

h, the holidays. Some are great excuses for a day (or 2, or 3, off)—some force you to spend way too much time with smelly Aunt Bea—but all of them are reasons to show off your bartending skills and celebrate with these party-ready cocktails. Can't stand watching the State of the Union Address, but know you really should? Have a few—or forty—friends over, break out the bottles, and whip up some Painkillers. Or spice up your Thanksgiving with a Pilgrim's Progress. Every day is a holiday—go ahead and celebrate them all!

CHAPTER 10

DANGER ZONE! DRINKS WITH EXTRA KICK

Sometimes all you want is a glass of wine. Or an ice-cold beer. Or a good old-fashioned root beer. And sometimes you're in the mood to really let your hair down and go for something a little more potent. Why not?

Maybe it's a special occasion. Did you get that long-awaited promotion you'd been angling for? Could it be a bachelorette party for your favorite party animal? Get ready to celebrate with a Tequila Bombshell and an Avalanche!

Then again, maybe you got dumped by that jerk you were dating for way too long. Maybe it's been a rough day at the office—for three weeks straight; or maybe you just gave your two-weeks' notice. We've all been there. Be shameless—throw yourself a pick-me-up party, and splurge!

Sure, these potent potables aren't for every day, and you should use 'em with care. But that's no reason not to whip them up every once in a while! Boilermakers, Zombies, the infamous Long Island Iced Tea—they're all right here. Beware, but *do* try these at home!

Boilermaker

Can't decide whether to have a beer or something stronger? Have both! Mixing beer and whiskey can be a tricky combination—but it works in moderation! We've heard of substituting vodka for the whiskey, but we prefer the old-fashioned way. Bottoms up!

1 bottle of beer   1½ ounces whiskey

Crack open the beer—preferably a pale ale, which has a full crisp taste without being heavy—and pour into a cold pint glass. Fill a shot glass with the whiskey and drop the whole thing right into the beer (gently!) and let the games begin.

Fireball

Great balls of fire! If you're a fan of all things hot and spicy, this one's for you. Guaranteed to make your ears smoke, it's just the thing when you're sick of syrupy-sweet shots and are craving something a little more daring. Another perk? It lets you leave the breath mints and chewing gum at home!

1½ ounces cinnamon schnapps   ½ ounce Goldschlager

Fill your cocktail shaker with ice and swirl the cinnamon schnapps into it. Shake it well and pour it into a shooter (a large 3-ounce shot glass). Top with Goldschlager for an extra touch of golden cinnamon, and get ready to breathe fire!

Texas Tequila Shot

We just had to include everyone's favorite let-your-hair-down drink! You know the routine when it comes to this do-it-yourself margarita, but have you ever tried licking the salt off his wrist, and vice versa? Makes things a little more interesting! And here's a spicy twist: Substitute an orange slice for the lemon, and cinnamon for the salt.

1½ ounces tequila
1 lemon slice
Sprinkle of salt

Let's get ready to rumble! Toss the tequila into a shot glass; grab a lemon slice; and set both aside. Lick your wrist, and sprinkle it liberally with salt. Then lick off the salt, swallow the tequila, and suck on the lemon. (Remember, if you do more than 1 shot, you're liable to miss work tomorrow morning!)

Tequila shots are par for the course at Coyote Ugly, a hot hole-in-the-wall of a honky-tonk joint in the East Village of Manhattan. (Yes, we saw the movie, and no, it wasn't filmed at the bar itself!) On request, the bar-dancing bartenders will even pour tequila into one of their cowboy boots, then serve it as a shot to a too-brave customer. Don't try this at home, though. When Megan hopped up onto the bar at C.U., the first thing she did was knock a speaker off of the top shelf!

Danger Zone! Drinks with Extra Kick

Long Island Iced Tea

ou've always wondered what the heck they put in Long Island Iced Tea. Well, there's no tea, that's for sure! This tricky drink tastes just like it, though; that's what makes them so addictive (and dangerous)! Whip up a batch at your next party. To take the edge off of their potency, pack the glass with ice before serving.

2 ounces vodka
1 ounce gin
1 ounce tequila
1 ounce rum
½ ounce white crème de menthe
2 ounces fresh lemon juice or sour mix
1 teaspoon sugar
1 shot of lemon-lime soda

Put your cocktail shaker to work; fill it with ice, then toss in the vodka, gin, tequila, rum, crème de menthe, lemon juice or sour mix, and sugar. Shake it up; then carefully pour it into a Collins glass over plenty of ice. Add a shot of lemon-lime soda at the end; then sit back and sip!

ZOMBIE

Once you've tried a Zombie, you'll know how it got its name! Three kinds of rum combine to make this creative cocktail a regular knockout. Its tropical taste makes it perfect for partying away long summer nights. You'll want to sip slowly, though, so you don't look like a walk-on for *Night of the Living Dead* in the morning!

2 ounces light rum
2 ounces dark rum
1 ounce overproof rum
1 ounce triple sec
½ ounce curaçao
1 ounce fresh lime juice

1 ounce fresh orange juice
1 ounce fresh pineapple juice
Dash of grenadine
1 pineapple spear, for garnish
1 orange slice, for garnish

Fill your cocktail shaker with ice; then add the light rum, dark rum, overproof rum, triple sec, curaçao, and juices. Give it a few good shakes; then strain it into a Collins glass over ice. Slip the pineapple and orange on the glass for the full effect—dangerously divine!

YOU'VE PROBABLY ONLY HAD IT WITH CORNED BEEF, BUT IT'S NOT JUST FOR ST. Patty's Day anymore! Cabbage has been lauded as an effective hangover remedy since ancient Rome—and, apparently, it prevents imbibers from becoming too tipsy in the first place. So *that's* why the Irish have a reputation for tough tolerances!

SKULL CRACKER

Think this little libation sounds wicked? Well, you're right. Between yummy pineapple juice and lip-licking white crème de cacao, you'll forget about the rum entirely. But you'll remember it in the morning when you've got a killer headache, unless you snack on light nibbles like Asian-style spring rolls, chicken skewers, or edamame. Eat, drink, and be merry!

3 ounces light rum
1 ounce white crème de cacao
1 ounce pineapple juice
1 ounce lemon juice

Pour the rum, white crème de cacao, pineapple juice, and lemon juice into your cocktail shaker over ice. Shake it up so the flavors blend beautifully, then strain into a Collins glass filled with ice. Truly tropical, completely cooling.

EVER WONDER HOW LIQUOR GOT THE UNLIKELY NICKNAME, BOOZE? WELL, legend has it that ancient Egyptians formed dried cakes of crushed grain, which could easily stand up to the heat of the desert for long periods of time. When dissolved in water, the grain would begin to ferment, making "instant beer" which they called *boozah*. (Convenient, no?) Okay, so this legend isn't documented on the Rosetta stone, but since Egyptians were the world's first brewers, we believe it!

PLANTER'S PUNCH

A southern specialty, Planter's Punch will deliver a much-needed attitude adjustment after a tough day when you mix it with good friends and a long Friday night. (Megan's buddy from Louisiana swears by the stuff—in moderation, of course!) We like to sip them while nibbling stress-free, easy-to-make appetizers such as guacamole with chips, mini pizzas, and other savory snacks.

1½ ounces light rum
2 ounces dark rum
¾ ounce bourbon
¾ ounce cognac
1 ounce lemon juice
1 teaspoon sugar
1–2 shots club soda

Grab that cocktail shaker, fill it with ice, and add the light rum, dark rum, bourbon, cognac, lemon juice, and sugar. Shake to mix and chill this cooling concoction; strain into a Collins glass over ice. Top with 1 or 2 shots of club soda—it's guaranteed to get the party started quickly!

TEQUILA BOMBSHELL

Boom! The Tequila Bombshell may not be as tough as a plain ol' shot of the stuff, but it still does a bang-up job of livening up any party. Southern Comfort and o.j. combined with tequila make a fun, fruity cocktail that'll get you ready to dance. If you're tired of margaritas, these are a great alternative.

1½ ounces tequila	1 ounce orange juice
1½ ounces Southern Comfort	2 lime slices

Swirl the tequila, Southern Comfort, orange juice, and 1 lime slice into your ice-filled cocktail shaker. Shake, shake, shake; strain into a cold cocktail glass. Slip a lime slice over the edge, and you're set!

AH, THE JOYS AND THE PAINS OF TEQUILA. IN MODERATION, IT'S SO GOOD; in excess, it's so, so bad. Take it from our friend Ryan, who went to Mexico with a bunch of friends on vacation. On the second night of their trip, she met a wildly attractive man, and sparks flew left and right. After a few margaritas, they went for a walk on the beach; but Ryan must have had just one too many. It wasn't long before she found herself under a catamaran making out with Mr. Wonderful—just minutes later, the Mexican police happened upon them and put an end to their, um, budding relationship. Unless you're a fan of Mexican jails, go easy on the tequila!

Annie Oakley

Just like the sharp-shooting cowgirl from whom this cocktail borrows its name, the Annie Oakley isn't all sugar and spice! If you're serving it at your next soiree, put one into the hand of that hot guy you've been dying to snog—he'll think it's a "girly" drink until both kinds of vodka kick in. Annie's one tough broad.

> 1 ounce raspberry vodka
> 2 ounces vanilla vodka
> 1 ounce light cream
> Dash of grenadine

Swirl the raspberry vodka, vanilla vodka, and light cream (calories be damned!) over ice in your cocktail shaker. Shake it up, strain it into a chilled cocktail glass, and drizzle blood-red grenadine on top. It's to die for!

DYLAN THOMAS

Named for the famous poet who liked whiskey (and the White Horse Tavern in New York City) a little too much, this tart, no-nonsense cocktail will be an inspiration to you, too. Girly mixers are tossed out the window in favor of minimalist whiskey and lemon juice (invest in some quality whiskey, since it's the star of this show).

3 ounces whiskey
½ ounce fresh lemon juice
Dash of sour mix

Toss the whiskey, lemon juice, and sour mix into your cocktail shaker; shake it up and strain into a well-chilled cocktail glass. Craving a sweet touch? Toss in a bright red maraschino cherry.

"One: I am a Welshman;
two: I am a drunkard;
and three: I am a lover of the
human race, especially women."
—Dylan Thomas

Avalanche

This pure-white drink looks innocent, and it slides down as easily as cold, fresh snow, but it's got a bite that grabs you by the throat. Chocolaty, minty, and perfectly potent, we like to enjoy them after dinner; that way, we can have a couple of them without worrying about feeling snowed-in tomorrow morning.

2 ounces vodka
1 ounce white crème de cacao
1 ounce white crème de menthe

Fill your cocktail shaker with plenty of ice—the Avalanche should be nothing less than ice cold! Add the vodka, crème de cacao, and crème de menthe, and shake well. Then strain it into a chilled cocktail glass—it's a wintery wonder.

VODKA, THE WATER OF LIFE. TODAY, BARS HAVE SEVERAL KINDS OF THE strong, clear stuff available, but it wasn't popular in the United States until the 1930s, when Smirnoff first opened its doors for business! Although many countries claim vodka as their own, it probably originated in Russia in the 13th century. Since it was thought to have a spirit of its own, it was often featured in Russian religious ceremonies. Later, it became customary to serve it at traditional banquets throughout the meal (much to the chagrin of visitors who might not be used to consuming as many as 13 shots of vodka with dinner), it's a tradition that still thrives to this day.

BLACKOUT

*I*f you've never tried Blackhaus, a potent raspberry brandy, you're missing out! Sure, it's strong, but the brilliant Blackout adds Chambord for a shot with a touch of sweetness. If you're sick of mixing up the same old Lemon Drops whenever you're in the mood for a sexy shooter, the Blackout will kick it up a notch.

1 ounce Blackhaus   ½ ounce Chambord

Put the Blackhaus in the freezer 3 hours before serving to chill it well. Grab a shot glass and fill it nearly full with Blackhaus. Pour the Chambord on top, and you're ready to rock and roll.

THERE'S NOTHING WORSE THAN BEING HUNG OVER ON A WORKDAY. YOU'RE AT your desk feeling queasy, your head's killing you—and you're supposed to be productive? Here are some tips for making it through:

- Keep a low profile. Don't advertise that hangover!
- Have a water bottle with you, and keep refilling it.
- If you can, correspond with business associates via e-mail, not phone. That way, you can reread your words and erase any mistakes your blurry mind might have caused.
- Keep an emergency late-night kit on hand in your desk drawer: include eye brightener, green cover-up stick to hide redness, moisturizer, face powder, and perfume. Don't forget the aspirin!
- Eat a protein-filled lunch. Does wonders for your tummy!
- Have a cup of caffeinated coffee—just one. That way, you'll feel less lethargic, but won't be buzzed and jittery.

CLIFFHANGER

There's a daredevil in all of us—let her out, and we bet she'll ask for a citrusy Cliffhanger. This distant cousin of the standard screwdriver is packed with extra punch in the guise of rum, curaçao, and sour mix. Whip up a whole pitcher—this recipe's great for doubling, tripling, or quadrupling—and you'll be the life of the party for sure.

1 ounce rum
1 ounce lemon vodka
1 ounce blue curaçao
2 ounces orange juice

3 ounces sour mix
1 lemon slice, for garnish
1 lime slice, for garnish

Toss the rum, lemon vodka, blue curaçao, orange juice, and sour mix into your handy ice-filled cocktail shaker. Shake it up (who says bartending isn't good exercise?) and pour it over fresh ice in a Collins glass. Slide the orange and lemon slices over the edge, and you're set.

DOING SOME DANCING IN DALLAS, DEBBIE? VISIT THE FUNKY **LIZARD Lounge**—2424 Swiss Avenue, (214) 826-4768—which even has a roofdeck with a gorgeous view of the Dallas skyline. And enjoy great Mexican fare at **Uncle Julio's**—4125 Lemmon Avenue, (214) 520-6620—the frozen cocktails (especially the margs!) are delish, and the food can't be beat. But did you expect anything else from Dallas?

Southern Sting

or bourbon lovers only! Surrounded by lip-puckering lemon juice and fresh peppermint schnapps, this cocky cocktail will hit you right in the kisser. Stronger than a Mint Julep, more powerful than a Whiskey Sour, the Southern Sting can leap tall buildings in a single bound. Are you ready to take it on?

2 ounces bourbon
1 ounce fresh lemon juice
½ ounce peppermint schnapps
1 teaspoon simple syrup (see page 58), or to taste
Sugar, to rim glass

Ouch! Toss the bourbon, lemon juice, peppermint schnapps, and simple syrup into your trusty cocktail shaker filled with ice. Shake until the simple syrup's dissolved and strain this little devil into sugar-rimmed cocktail glasses.

NOSEDIVE

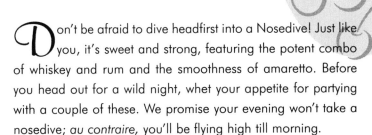

on't be afraid to dive headfirst into a Nosedive! Just like you, it's sweet and strong, featuring the potent combo of whiskey and rum and the smoothness of amaretto. Before you head out for a wild night, whet your appetite for partying with a couple of these. We promise your evening won't take a nosedive; *au contraire,* you'll be flying high till morning.

2 ounces whiskey
1 ounce rum
1 ounce amaretto
1 maraschino cherry, for garnish

This cocktail takes just seconds. Toss the whiskey, rum, and amaretto into an ice-filled cocktail shaker and shake it up, baby. Strain into a cold cocktail glass, pop in 1 or 2 cherries, and put your dancing shoes on!

> *"Sir, if you were my husband,*
> *I would poison your drink."*
> —Lady Astor to Winston Churchill
> *"Madam, if you were my wife,*
> *I would drink it."*
> —Churchill's reply

DANGER ZONE! DRINKS WITH EXTRA KICK

After reading Chapter 10, you might be thinking, "Whew, these women are hard-core. What gives?" Never fear, we're fans of responsible drinking only, but Danger Zone drinks are lots of fun when you just have one or two. They're best for the little celebrations in life, like "I finally quit that awful job!" or "I finally snagged an interview with the best company in the world!" or even the ever-popular, "I just feel like celebrating!" We love a sweet Skull Cracker, a take-no-prisoners Fireball, and a well-made Long Island Iced Tea, but we also advocate switching to booze-free treats before the world gets fuzzy. Cheers!

CHAPTER 11

THAT'S TOO SEXY!

When you're offered an Alabama Slammer, you wonder what slamming has to do with Alabama and you can't help blushing. When your best friend calmly asks for a Buttery Nipple shot at a bar, you're amazed. And you turn cranberry-red when the hot guy you've been talking to all night offers you a Sex on the Beach.

Does this describe you? If so, you might want to proceed into this chapter with caution! It's packed with wild concoctions with wilder names that you'd hardly dare ask a bartender for. There's something here to make even the most brazen babe blush.

That makes these wicked cocktails just right for a bachelorette party, perfect preludes to a great girls' night out, or torturous tools for bribery ("If you don't order me a Screaming Orgasm right now, I'm going to march right up to you know who and tell him you know what!"). Not that we promote extortion, of course. At least, not usually.

See for yourself! Choose your favorite passionately titled poison . . . we're sure you'll be, um, satisfied.

SCREAMING ORGASM

Remember Meg Ryan in *When Harry Met Sally?* Well, now you can have what she's having! This decadent cocktail is so good, it's better than . . . anything you've ever had before! Try it tonight as an after-dinner drink or your first drink of the evening. You'll want to whip up a few again, and again, and again . . .

1½ ounces vodka
1 ounce Kahlua
1 ounce Irish cream

Fill an Old-Fashioned glass half full with ice, toss in the vodka, Kahlua, and Irish cream, and pour everything into your cocktail shaker to mix well. Return the mixture to an Old-Fashioned glass (ice included). Was it good for you?

"When she raises her eyelids it's as if she were taking off all her clothes."
—Sidonie Gabrielle Claudine Colette

CLIMAX

*Y*our evening will peak after you've tried a Climax, which, in this case, is like a liquid banana split. If you've having a bachelorette party, this wickedly sweet, sexy libation is not to be missed! Its seductive sweetness will put you all in the mood for a rockin' good time. (Or, for extra laughs, you could insist that the bride-to-be order it by name!)

1 ounce vodka
½ ounce amaretto
½ ounce white crème de cacao
½ ounce crème de banana
Dash of cream

Grab your cocktail shaker, toss in the vodka, amaretto, white crème de cacao, and crème de banana, and give it a few good shakes to mix. Gently strain it into a cocktail glass. Satisfaction guaranteed!

WE KNOW, WE KNOW, LOS ANGELES HAS SO MANY FABULOUS NIGHTSPOTS it's impossible to pick just a few favorites! But for a smoky, sexy, romantic atmosphere, it's hard to beat **Daddy's Lounge**—1610 Vine Street, (323) 463-7777—a prime hookup joint. Or indulge in a massive martini at **Liquid Kitty**—11780 West Pico Boulevard, (310) 473-3707—and enjoy its laid-back attitude (unless it's a Saturday night, of course).

ANGEL'S TIT

Believe it or not, the Angel's Tit is quite a classic. We're not quite sure how it got its creative handle, but it's probably because it makes you feel like you've gone straight to heaven after having only one. If you love chocolate-covered cherries, this one's especially for you; if not, it'll make you a believer—guaranteed.

¼ ounce white crème de cacao
¼ ounce maraschino liqueur

¼ ounce light cream
1 maraschino cherry, for garnish

In a shot glass, layer the white crème de cacao, the maraschino liqueur, and the cream. Top the sexy shooter with a cherry.

HARD AND HARDER

Midori: These days it's not just for Melon Balls. This drink mixes just the right amount of Midori with orangey curaçao and versatile vodka to make a turquoise cocktail that's just the thing when you want something fruity, yet sweetish and strong—a quirky take on a straight-up margarita.

2 ounces vodka
1 ounce Midori

¾ ounce blue curaçao
Dash of sour mix

Fill your cocktail shaker with ice and toss the vodka, Midori, blue curaçao, and sour mix over it. (It's already the most colorful cocktail you've ever had!) Shake, shake, shake, and strain into a chilled cocktail glass. Sinfully sweet and tart!

BETWEEN THE SHEETS

*I*t's true, this drink is the next best thing! Mix up a couple for that new guy you're dating. This potent potion is dangerous, since it's 80 percent unadulterated booze! (We recommend a cold glass of water as a chaser.)

2 ounces cognac

1 ounce light rum

1 ounce white curaçao

½ ounce fresh lemon juice

1 or 2 lemon slices

Fill your cocktail shaker with ice and swirl the cognac, light rum, curaçao, and lemon juice over it. Shake it up—it's especially important to mix the flavors well in this drink—then strain it into a chilled cocktail glass. Slip 1 or 2 lemon slices over the edge, and you're in for the night!

CHI-CHI

*M*eaning "swank" in French and "breasts" in Spanish, this drink tastes like a sultry summer evening. And who can resist anything made with pineapple juice? Not us!

2 ounces rum

4 ounces pineapple juice

1 ounce brandy

1 pineapple spear, for garnish

No shaker needed! Fill a Collins glass with ice cubes and add the rum and pineapple juice. Stir, float the brandy on top, and slip a pineapple spear over the edge. *Ai, mami!*

THAT'S TOO SEXY!

SLIPPERY NIPPLE

ou've had them at every party, every girls-only outing, and countless other times, too. But how do you *make* them? There are numerous recipes, but ours keeps it simple. Sambuca, which smacks of fennel, works surprisingly well with Irish cream's rich, creamy quality and grenadine adds attitude. We dare you to ask for one at your favorite watering hole!

2 ounces sambuca   Drizzle of grenadine
1 ounce Irish cream

No ice necessary for this lickable libation! Just make sure the sambuca and the cocktail glass are well chilled. Pour the sambuca into the cocktail glass and float the Irish cream on top. Drizzle with grenadine and you've got a cocktail with more kick than you'll know what to do with!

SO YOUR BEST FRIEND'S GETTING MARRIED? A BACHELORETTE PARTY IS IN order, of course! Here's everything you'll need to make it a night she'll never forget. First, several bottles of good champagne, for celebrating at your house over appetizers. Then, a faux veil to wear while bar-hopping, so the whole world will know she'll soon be a bride. And don't forget an outrageous feather boa, to up the embarrassment factor. Finally, send her on a scavenger hunt—she'll have to kiss one man who's under the age of twenty-one, have three men buy her drinks, and so on; or she won't get her gifts at the end of the evening!

BLOW JOB

$\mathcal{M}$ore fun than the real thing and more decadent than an ice-cream sundae, this fun-to-drink shot is always a hit at parties. Sure, the Irish cream and vodka are a great combination, but the whipped cream is really what this drink's all about. Some especially skilled friends of ours can kick them back using only their teeth, but we're too afraid of swallowing the shot glass *and* the shot.

½ ounce vodka
½ ounce Irish cream
Dollop whipped cream

It's easy to make the drink that's the star of bachelorette parties everywhere! Pour the chilled vodka into a shot glass and add the Irish cream on top. Add as much whipped cream as you can handle . . . then add more! Finally, kick the whole thing back—using your hands is optional.

"Eat, drink, and be merry,
for tomorrow you may have
maxed out your credit card."
—Megan Buckley

SEX ON A SNOWY BEACH

*Y*ikes! The name might strike fear into your heart as you imagine frostbite, blue lips, and a pleasant case of pneumonia, but trust us, the drink tastes much better! Sex on a Snowy Beach is so easy to make, and will warm the cockles of your heart in hot and cold weather alike. Whip up a pitcher this Friday night!

1 can frozen orange juice
3 ounces peach schnapps
1 can vodka (use the orange juice can to measure)
1 can water (use the orange juice can to measure)
3–4 peach slices, for garnish

You won't be cold for long! Toss everything into your blender (isn't that orange juice can the handiest measurement ever?) and blend until the mixture is icy smooth. Pour into Old-Fashioned glasses and slide peach slices over the edges for extra sass. (Makes a full pitcher, so you'll have plenty to share!)

SLOE SCREW

Oh, stop! We're talking about a *drink*, girls. Forgo your usual screwdriver—vodka and orange juice—for something a little more creative! This basic, brilliant recipe can be reworked into tons of fun variations, such as a Sloe, Comfortable Screw (just add Southern Comfort) or a Sloe, Comfortable, Fuzzy Screw (add Southern Comfort and peach schnapps). We like the original, though!

3 ounces sloe gin	1 orange slice, for garnish
3 ounces orange juice	1 lemon slice, for garnish

Fill your cocktail shaker with ice and swirl the sloe gin and orange juice over it. Shake well and pour the whole mix (including the ice) into a Collins glass. Pop 1 orange slice and 1 lemon slice over the edge and you've got a screwdriver with extra attitude!

WHAT THE HECK IS SLOE GIN? YOU'VE SEEN IT IN DRINKS HERE AND THERE, but did you know it's not gin at all? It's actually a sweet, gin-based liqueur that's flavored with blackthorn, or *sloe*, plums. It's great when combined with citrusy mixers like orange or lemon juice, or in tandem with vodka or rum, and you've seen it in drinks like the Alabama Slammer. There's just one caveat, though, don't make a martini with the stuff!

MARQUIS DE SADE

on't worry, this won't hurt! In fact, this daring little drink will do just the opposite. Named for the infamous French writer, it's both sweet and tart and it packs the extra punch that overproof rum offers. (Be careful you don't go over-board, though!) Pop a cherry on top and you've got the sexiest cocktail this side of the Atlantic.

2½ ounces vodka
1 ounce Chambord
½ ounce overproof rum
Dash of sour mix
1 maraschino cherry, for garnish

This one takes no prisoners! Grab your ice-filled cocktail shaker and toss the vodka, Chambord, rum, and sour mix into it. Shake it up, strain it into a chilled cocktail glass, and add the cherry. A little pain can be yummy!

MANY HAVE CALLED THE MARQUIS DE SADE THE MOST INFAMOUS WRITER IN the history of French literature—and with good reason. A complex character, he was a revolutionary novelist and philosopher of the late 18th century—and a criminal, to boot. Want to know more? *Quills,* a graphic but excellent film starring Jeffrey Rush, Michael Caine, and Kate Winslet illustrates the fascinating life and times of the Marquis.

MASSAGE

Skip the overpriced backrub! Instead, kick back and relax with our version! The ultimate drink for citrus lovers. The Massage soothes weary taste buds with both lemon vodka *and* limon rum and the dash of grenadine makes the whole thing as pretty as a tequila sunrise. This drink's a guaranteed people-pleaser—don't be afraid to mix up a few for your next shindig.

2 ounces lemon vodka	1 ounce orange juice
1 ounce limon rum	Dash of grenadine

This one'll rub you the right way! Swirl the vodka, rum, orange juice, and grenadine over ice in your cocktail shaker. After a few good shakes, strain it into a chilled cocktail glass. Drizzle a few drops of grenadine on top and get ready to de-stress.

SOUTH AFRICAN AND NATIVE AMERICAN CULTURES SWEAR THAT EATING A FEW nuts, such as almonds or peanuts, will prevent you from feeling flat tomorrow morning. Go ahead and grab a couple of handfuls of mixed nuts from the bowl on the bar, or have a peanut butter sandwich before heading out for the evening. At the very least, you'll have something in your stomach to help absorb a couple of cocktails, and you won't have to go to bed hungry. So go ahead and go nuts!

THAT'S TOO SEXY!

A LITTLE SATISFACTION

*I*n spite of what a famous man once said, now you *can* get some—especially if you've got a sweet tooth. A Little Satisfaction is easy to come by with just three ingredients, and it's well proportioned. It's half crystal-clear vodka and half sweet, complementary liqueurs. We admit it, it's a girly drink, so save for a ladies-only event.

    2 ounces vodka, chilled
    1 ounce Frangelico
    1 ounce Irish cream
    1 maraschino cherry, for garnish

We promise it'll satisfy your senses! Toss the vodka and Frangelico into your ice-filled cocktail shaker, shake well to make sure it's chilled, and strain it into a cold cocktail glass. Float the Irish cream on top and pop a maraschino cherry into the mix. You'll be asking for more!

Cold Shower

*Y*ou want a drink that's refreshing, but you're not in the mood for an ultra-sweet concoction, you've never been a fan of fruit juice mixers, and you're just not feeling an average martini tonight. The solution? A Cold Shower! Gin and vodka balance each other perfectly, surrounding sweetly crisp crème de menthe, and a dash of club soda adds sparkle. Just what you were looking for!

1½ ounces gin   Dash of club soda
1½ ounces vodka   1 fresh mint sprig, for garnish
1 ounce white crème de menthe

Rough and refreshing! Grab your cocktail shaker, fill it with ice, then toss the gin, vodka, and crème de menthe over it. Shake it up and strain it into a chilled cocktail glass. A dash of club soda completes the deal. Pop a fresh mint sprig over the edge for fun, or serve straight up.

IT'S ONE OF THE OLDEST TALL TALES ABOUT BOOZE—STEPPING INTO A COLD shower sobers you up. Just like black coffee, it might make you feel better (it probably will!); but then again, anything that's not another drink is almost guaranteed to do the same thing. Girls, you've heard it time and again, and it's true: The only thing that'll remedy a few too many cocktails is time. (Several glasses of water and a brisk walk won't do any harm, though!)

THAT'S TOO SEXY!

Fuzzy Chocolate Nut

D on't get the wrong idea about this one! No kidding, the Fuzzy Chocolate Nut gets its name simply from its ingredient list. Peach schnapps adds peach "fuzz," amaretto adds "nuttiness," and hot chocolate adds, well, chocolate. Sound unusual? It is, but it works, and it's just the thing to sweeten a long, cold winter night. Plus, it packs a surprisingly small punch.

4 ounces hot chocolate
1½ ounces peach schnapps
½ ounce amaretto
Dollop whipped cream
Sprinkle of ground cinnamon, for garnish
Sprinkle of chocolate shavings, for garnish

Fill a warm mug with hot chocolate, then add the peach schnapps and amaretto. Stir and top with as much whipped cream as you'd like. Sprinkle ground cinnamon and chocolate shavings over the whipped cream, or skip the frills and serve straight.

$\mathcal{I}$t's happened to all of us—you approach the bartender, and say ever so casually, "Yeah, I'd like a Blow Job, please?" and instead of simply serving you the drink, he a) teases you mercilessly; b) points you out to every guy in the bar; and c) remembers you as *the Blow Job girl* every time he sees you. Well, we're sure this chapter has toughened you up! Did you try a Climax, a Slippery Nipple, or a Between the Sheets? If you serve them at your next party, make your guests ask for them by name. No exceptions! ("I'm sorry, I didn't hear you. Did you ask for a *Screaming Orgasm*?! Oh. Okay.")

INDEX

U, V

Uncle Julio's, 161
V Bar, 94
Velvet Lounge, 94
Vermouth, 4, 43, 44, 84, 89
Vodka, 159; Amarettopolitan, 112;
Annie Oakley, 157; Avalanche,
159; Bloody Mary, 113; Blow
Job, 171; Candy Bar Cocktail,
145; Cape Cod in Winter, 68;
Champagne Sangria, 141;
Cherry Alive, 130; Cherry Tree
Martini, 136; Classic
Cosmopolitan, The, 100;
Cliffhanger, 161; Climax, 167;
Cocopolitan, 103; Cointreau
Cosmo, 101; Cold Shower, 177;
Cosmic Cosmo, 102;
Cosmopolitan Mandarin Martini,
114; Creamsicle, 61; Cupid's
Elixir, 135; Fuzzy Buzzy, 140;
Hamptons, The, 58; Hard and
Harder, 168; Harvey Wallbanger,
46; Hot and Dirty Martinis, 121;
Jazzberry Cosmo, 106; Kissing
Fool, A, 113; Little Satisfaction,
A, 176; Long Island Iced Tea,
152; Marquis de Sade, 174;
martinis, 2, 6–9; Massage, 175;
Mexicosmopolitan, 108; Million-
Dollar Melon Ball, 109; Mint
Condition, 92; Mudslide, 118;
Pacific Rim Cocktail, 54;
Painkiller, 134; Peaches and
Cream Cosmo, 105; Pilgrim's
Progress, 146; Raspberry Cooler,
65; Room for Two, A, 123;
Screaming Orgasm, 166;
Strawberry Liplicker, 59; That
Little Tart, 107; Watermelon
Cosmopolitan, 104; White
Russian, 91

W

Warm Apple Cider, 73
Watermelon Cosmopolitan, 104
Whipped cream, 79
Whiskey: Boilermaker, 150; Dylan
Thomas, 158; Hot Toddy, 70;
Irish Coffee, 68; Irish Temper,
The, 137; Manhattan, 43;
Nosedive, 163; Shirley Temple
and the Devil, 36
White Russian, 91
White Velvet Kisses, 126
Windjammer, 49
Wine: Gluhwein, 69; Sangria, 64

Z

Zombie, 153

ABOUT THE AUTHORS

Sheree Bykofsky is a top New York literary agent and the author of 17 books, including *The 52 Most Romantic Dates in and Around New York City* and *The Complete Idiot's Guide to Getting Published* (2nd edition). She lives in Manhattan and teaches publishing at New York University.

Megan Buckley has worked on the assembly line at General Motors, at a convent, at more than one publishing company, and is now pursuing a career as a literary agent and freelance writer. She's been a guest bartender, and when no one's looking, she tends bar at her local pub on the east side of Manhattan.